MINDING THE MONEY

An Investment Guide for Nonprofit Board Members

Robert P. Fry, Jr.

BOARDSOURCE
Building Effective Nonprofit Boards

Formerly the National Center for Nonprofit Boards

Library of Congress Cataloging-in-Publication Data

Fry, Robert P.
  Minding the money : an investment guide for nonprofit board
members / by Robert P. Fry, Jr.
      p. cm.
  Updated and enl. ed. of: Creating and using investment policies.
  ISBN 1-58686-075-5 (pbk., cd-rom)
 1. Nonprofit organizations--United States--Finance--Management.
2. Investments--United States. 3. Asset-liability management--
United States. 4. Nonprofit organizations--Law and legislation--
United States. I. Fry, Robert P. Creating and using investment poli-
cies. II. Title.
  HG4027.65.F788 2004
  658.15'2--dc22
                                                    2004007233

Published by BoardSource
1828 L Street, NW, Suite 900
Washington, DC 20036

Formerly the National Center for Nonprofit Boards

BoardSource, formerly the National Center for Nonprofit Boards, is the premier resource for practical information, tools and best practices, training, and leadership development for board members of nonprofit organizations worldwide. Through our highly acclaimed programs and services, BoardSource enables organizations to fulfill their missions by helping build strong and effective nonprofit boards.

BoardSource provides assistance and resources to nonprofit leaders through workshops, training, and our extensive Web site, www.boardsource.org. A team of BoardSource governance consultants works directly with nonprofit leaders to design specialized solutions to meet organizations' needs and assists nongovernmental organizations around the world through partnerships and capacity building. As the world's largest, most comprehensive publisher of materials on nonprofit governance, BoardSource offers a wide selection of books, videotapes, and CDs. BoardSource also hosts the BoardSource Leadership Forum, bringing together approximately 800 governance experts, board members, and chief executives of nonprofit organizations from around the world.

Created out of the nonprofit sector's critical need for governance guidance and expertise, BoardSource is a 501(c)(3) nonprofit organization that has provided practical solutions to nonprofit organizations of all sizes in diverse communities. In 2001, BoardSource changed its name from the National Center for Nonprofit Boards to better reflect its mission. Today, BoardSource has more than 15,000 members and has served more than 75,000 nonprofit leaders.

For more information, please visit our Web site, www.boardsource.org, e-mail us at mail@boardsource.org, or call us at 800-883-6262.

Have You Used These BoardSource Resources?

VIDEOS

Meeting the Challenge: An Orientation to Nonprofit Board Service

Speaking of Money: A Guide to Fund-Raising for Nonprofit Board Members

BOOKS

The Board Chair Handbook

Managing Conflicts of Interest: Practical Guidelines for Nonprofit Boards

Driving Strategic Planning: A Nonprofit Executive's Guide

The Board-Savvy CEO: How To Build a Strong, Positive Relationship with Your Board

Presenting: Board Orientation

Presenting: Nonprofit Financials

The Board Meeting Rescue Kit: 20 Ideas for Jumpstarting Your Board Meetings

The Board Building Cycle: Nine Steps to Finding, Recruiting, and Engaging Nonprofit Board Members

The Policy Sampler: A Resource for Nonprofit Boards

To Go Forward, Retreat! The Board Retreat Handbook

Nonprofit Board Answer Book: Practical Guide for Board Members and Chief Executives

Nonprofit Board Answer Book II: Beyond the Basics

The Legal Obligations of Nonprofit Boards

Self-Assessment for Nonprofit Governing Boards

Assessment of the Chief Executive

Fearless Fundraising

The Nonprofit Board's Guide to Bylaws

Understanding Nonprofit Financial Statements

Transforming Board Structure: New Possibilities for Committees and Task Forces

THE GOVERNANCE SERIES

1. *Ten Basic Responsibilities of Nonprofit Boards*

2. *Financial Responsibilities of Nonprofit Boards*

3. *Structures and Practices of Nonprofit Boards*

4. *Fundraising Responsibilities of Nonprofit Boards*

5. *Legal Responsibilities of Nonprofit Boards*

6. *The Nonprofit Board's Role in Setting and Advancing the Mission*

7. *The Nonprofit Board's Role in Planning and Evaluation*

8. *How To Help Your Board Govern More and Manage Less*

9. *Leadership Roles in Nonprofit Governance*

For an up-to-date list of publications and information about current prices, membership, and other services, please call BoardSource at 800-883-6262 or visit our Web site at www.boardsource.org.

Contents

CD-ROM: The CD attached to the inside back cover includes all appendices. The content can be downloaded and/or customized for distribution to board members, staff members, and chief executives. Additionally, individual state statute adoptions can be accessed via the World Wide Web with provided access links.

Preface

This guide is an update and expansion of an earlier version, also published by BoardSource, under the title *Creating and Using Investment Policies, a Guide for Nonprofit Boards*. I have received many kind comments from readers and users of that guide and shockingly little criticism! Thank you all.

In the interim, I also wrote a more extensive book on the same subject: *Nonprofit Investment Policies: Practical Steps for Growing Charitable Funds* (290 pages). The publisher, John Wiley & Sons, has graciously allowed me to excerpt passages from that book in this guide. Those of you wishing to read more detailed discussions of the concepts presented here may find the longer book useful.

Since the first publication of this guide, I moved to Merrill Lynch. For most of the past six years, I have worked for the Merrill Lynch Trust Company either serving high net-worth clients or, more recently, helping the Trust Company itself supervise the investment of its trust assets. In these roles, I have learned a great deal about the honorable work of being a trustee and the enormous burden of responsibility one assumes in that role. I have also been taught, encouraged, and assisted by my many friends and colleagues at Merrill Lynch. Despite their invaluable help, I have managed to develop opinions that differ, at times, from the norms in the industry. All such opinions — and any errors — are entirely my own.

While many people at BoardSource were very helpful with comments and suggestions, I would like to thank Dennis Bass, Deputy Director at the Center for Science in the Public Trust, for his patient and helpful work in editing this text.

Finally, I want to acknowledge the contribution to this book of my 19-year-old daughter, Katie. While I was working on it, Katie made her first mutual fund investments. Several weeks later, she called me on my cell phone. Since she was calling during the day from her college in New York, I excused myself from a business meeting to answer the call. Katie said excitedly, "Guess what, Dad? My mutual fund is up $75!"

Investing is a serious business and supervising investments as a trustee is more serious still. But investing, as Katie discovered, can also be a lot of fun. I hope this book will help you avoid many of the problems and pitfalls that can take the fun out of investing, and will provide the personal satisfaction that comes from serving your chosen charity well.

Robert P. Fry, Jr.

Introduction:
Who's Minding the Money?

The purpose of this book is to help members of a nonprofit board supervise the investment of financial assets held or controlled by the organization. I have tried to discuss each issue from the perspective of a trustee or director, focusing on that which is unique in the nonprofit world and on board members' fiduciary responsibilities. In doing so, I have assumed a basic knowledge of investment concepts on the part of the reader. (But for those who would like a thorough discussion of investment basics, my personal favorite is *A Random Walk Down Wall Street,* by Burton Malkiel, first published in 1973 and now in its 8th edition.) The discussions that follow assume the reader understands fundamental investment concepts apart from the fiduciary context. Thus, we are not going to cover the definitions of stocks and bonds; the operation of the markets; the normal business functions of banks, brokers, and other advisors; or the fundamentals of corporate finance.

Perhaps the first "money" question in the nonprofit world is: Who's in charge? Surprisingly, the answer is not always obvious. As in many for-profit businesses, executives frequently think and act as if they are completely in charge. Often, in fact, they are — because the board has taken no interest in investment decisions. Sometimes major donors believe they are in control, by virtue of the power that derives from their financial support. Even when such donors have no legal authority over the organization's funds, a degree of them nonetheless exercise *de facto* control over investment decisions. Finally, there is the occasional nonprofit organization that is controlled by third parties; community foundations are examples of this model.

In virtually every case, however, *legal* responsibility for supervising organizational investments resides squarely with the board of directors. Investment authority can reside functionally somewhere else, but it must be shaped, guided, and constrained by an informed board operating with well-designed policies and procedures. Otherwise, it may become a legal nightmare in which the board members incur personal liability for the actions of people they do not supervise or manage.

The fundamental challenge for board members is to find the proper balance between their legal responsibilities and the practical needs of the organization. The executive staff, for example, is in charge of the organization's daily operations. The chief executive often works closely with the board and has much to contribute to the discussion of investments, as do major donors, other staff, and outside advisors. The board needs their help, but it must not abdicate its responsibilities.

With effective and appropriate entrustment, a board can encourage creativity, delegation of authority, team work, community spirit, and a common vision. But a board must successfully supervise all these parties. To do that, there are at least two key requirements: knowledgeable board members and appropriate policies and procedures.

Why Invest?

Since investing seems to bring with it all kinds of problems and issues, another reasonable "first" question is: Why invest at all?

The most salient answer is that investing is simply good stewardship. Being a good steward of an organization's assets is a responsibility that comes with participation on a nonprofit board. A more practical answer is that investing is *unavoidable*. Any surplus, even cash in a non–interest-bearing checking account, is "invested," from the financial world's perspective. It is invested because the organization, as the owner of the funds, is allowing another institution — a bank — to hold its funds in exchange for a return, which in this example is the provision of checking services. While that might not be a good investment — as the organization may well be able to get checking services *and* an interest payment on its funds — it is nonetheless an investment.

At some point in its life, a board must consciously and deliberately invest if it is to properly discharge its duty. There are at least four reasons why this is the case: inflation, opportunities for growth, the relative cost of fundraising, and something I call "worthiness."

Inflation

The insidiousness of inflation is that it depreciates the value of cash. If one holds currency or cash equivalents during a period in which there is any inflation at all, the purchasing power, and therefore the true value of an asset, declines. Allowing something to unnecessarily decline in value is wasteful.

In a noninflationary environment the failure to invest funds results in lost opportunities, but not true economic losses. Money in the bank at 2 percent still generates a real return of 2 percent. But adding inflation to the mix can be lethal: A mere 3 percent inflation rate means that a 2 percent interest-bearing bank account results in a true economic loss of 1 percent per year. Even in a very low-inflation economy, if a board fails to invest its surplus, it effectively allows those funds to waste away over time. This is not good stewardship.

Inflation compels a board to invest as a means of caring for and preserving the value of its assets. The fact that investments in U.S. treasury bills (interest-bearing government notes with a term of one year or less) have kept up with inflation over the last 50 years might lead a board to believe that it could have its cake and eat it too — investing in a safe, conservative instrument that also protects the organization's funds from inflationary depreciation. That might be true, *if* the organization is not spending any of the funds. But if the board wishes both to maintain purchasing power *and* spend some of the money, it will have to invest in other ways.

Opportunities for Growth

A second reason to invest a nonprofit's assets is to exploit the growth potential that the funds represent. As an organization accumulates cash, it has a wonderful opportunity to increase revenues and decrease pressure on fundraising by maximizing its investment returns. An extra 3 or 4 percent of total return can, over the years, make an enormous difference in the financial health and asset base of an organization. Because we earn investment returns without marketing costs, any improvement in investment performance directly benefits the organization.

THE TRUE COST OF FUNDRAISING

Fundraising costs in the nonprofit world tend to be understated. No matter how accurate the accounting of fundraising expenses, that accounting rarely (if ever) captures all of the fundraising costs, which include the "lost opportunity" costs of the time, effort, and energy that raising funds can drain from staff, executives, and board members. Additional funds from investment returns can reduce the fundraising pressures on the organization's staff and supporters, freeing them to spend their time and emotional energy elsewhere. It is poor stewardship for a board not to ease the strain on an organization by maximizing the return on its investment assets.

WORTHINESS

Lastly, there is a concept that I term *worthiness*. Nonprofits characteristically entreat others to join them in a cause or altruistic mission by supporting the organization with gifts of time, talent, or treasure. Employees who work for nonprofits often make a significant personal contribution by choosing a lower-paying career track. The sacrifices that a nonprofit asks of others requires that the governing board make its best effort to protect, expand, and wisely invest the organizational assets.

Investment funds are an asset, just like a building or a piece of equipment, from which we can expect intangible benefits in addition to the normal returns of income or capital gains. Most importantly, holding substantial investment assets can convey the same sense of long-term commitment and permanence that an individual derives from owning his or her own home. Endowments convey to the world — and especially to potential donors of major gifts — that an organization plans to be there for the long haul. When those funds are well managed, and a commitment to good management is made public through the organization's policies and procedures, the worthiness of the entire organization is heightened. What a wonderful way to encourage and affirm the commitments we ask of others.

The following chapters contain information intended to help nonprofit board members supervise the creation of an investment process, and then reflect that process in the organization's investment policies. The material includes a discussion of portfolio theory for board members, as well as an overview of the legal environment in which charitable organizations invest their funds. It will also examine hiring advisors and monitoring their performance. Along the way, there is advice on appropriate board and committee structures as they relate to investing an organization's funds. The book concludes with a discussion of current investment issues. In the appendices you will find a sample set of policies, a copy of applicable laws, a sample self-guided investment audit, and a glossary of investment terms. Also, in the attached CD-ROM, you will find downloadable and customizable versions of each appendix, including Web-linked availability to applicable statutes in the tables of adopting jurisdictions.

1.
The Basics: First Steps for a Board

Several years before the dot-com bust and the major stock-market declines that followed, I wrote that "the investment environment today is innovative, accessible, and overwhelmingly friendly to the success of charitable participants" as a result of which "there is no longer any reason for a charitable organization of any size to fail to participate in the securities market in a measured and disciplined way."[1]

While that statement may seem odd, given the investment carnage that followed, it was true then — and is true today. The investment world is wide open in the sense that an organization with almost any amount of funds can participate on a fairly level playing field. The advantages held by the big investors, the insiders, and the powers of the industry, while real, nonetheless pale in comparison to the value of good judgment and a steady hand. Investing is truly an equal-opportunity venture.

But investing is not easy. It is an inherently risky enterprise in which the willingness to take a risk is part of why others are willing to pay you a return for the use of your money. It can also be a confusing world of too many choices that, at times, all sound the same. So before dealing with fiduciary and nonprofit investment issues, we need to look at the preliminary questions that governing boards should ask themselves:

- What assets are available to be managed?

- What are the investment goals, time frames, and restrictions?

- What is the board's tolerance for risk?

- What structures and policies need to be created to reach the board's goals?

While the boardroom is the appropriate venue to discuss and decide these questions, the board members do not need to do all, or even most, of the actual work. As is normal in a corporate structure, board members may properly use and rely upon both executive staff and outside advisors. But in each of these areas, board members must make the critical decisions and set the tone for the investment environment. That leadership is uniquely a board function.

IDENTIFYING ASSETS TO BE MANAGED

The first of the basics is determining exactly what assets an organization has to manage. Frequently, nonprofit organizations own or control far more in the way of financial assets than they initially realize. In part this is because assets may exist in different places and forms. Some of the more common categories of investable assets include

- operating reserves

- retirement funds

---

1. Fry, Robert P. Jr. *Nonprofit Investment Policies: Practical Steps for Growing Charitable Funds.* New York: John Wiley & Sons, 1998.

- capital campaign reserves

- endowments and foundations

In addition, some organizations are the beneficiaries of various planned gifts, which can include trusts, annuities, and pooled-income funds. Each of these categories of funds is different in terms of the time frames during which they must be managed, the purposes for which they are being held, the income or growth goals, and the levels of risk that should be taken. Identifying the funds an organization controls, its responsibility for them, and the character of the funds are the first of the basics.

When categorizing funds, a board should be cognizant of the difference between operating reserves and funds that are available for longer term investment. The board should solicit the analysis and advice of the chief executive and chief financial officer to determine how much money constitutes a reasonable operating surplus for the organization. Typically, that would be expressed in terms of months of operations. Most nonprofits use anywhere from three to 12 months as a benchmark, depending upon cash flows. An organization with wide fluctuations in cash flow or receivables will need larger operating reserves than an organization with consistent income.

Funds in an operating reserve are typically held in extremely liquid form so the organization is able to access its cash as needed. The most common structure is a checking account linked with a money market mutual fund or account. Such a structure typically "sweeps" daily balances from checking to money funds so that the reserves are always earning interest. Cash above and beyond the reserve amount is then available for longer term investment. Those funds should be invested quite differently from the operating reserve. Appendix V provides a self-assessment tool to help identify and categorize a nonprofit organization's assets.

SETTING INVESTMENT GOALS, TIME FRAMES, AND RESTRICTIONS

Making decisions about investing assets requires that a board assess the context within which the decisions are to be made. In the investment world, that context includes

- the goals for which the board is investing (e.g., growth, current income, or preservation of capital);

- the time frames available; and

- any specific restrictions or limitations on the organization or its funds.

Goals and time frames are commonly identified at the fund level. With operating reserves, for example, typical objectives would be to preserve capital, maintain complete liquidity, and earn whatever level of interest is possible without violating the first two objectives. Since the operating-reserve time frame is usually "right now," the goals for these funds will generally mandate investment in a checking account, money market fund, or other, comparable instrument.

At the other end of the spectrum, the goal for an organization's endowment funds would likely be to increase the fund as much as possible in anticipation of future spending. In that case, the time frame is essentially open ended and the current spending requirement is nonexistent. Within those criteria, the funds can be invested as aggressively as the risk tolerance of the board (discussed below) will allow.

Capital campaign funds fall in the middle. They often represent monies for which growth is fine, but not essential, and for which there is no current income requirement. However, the entire sum will probably be spent at a specific point in time, and so a portfolio of medium-term, fixed-income investments is likely to best suit those criteria.

For each of these examples, the board provides to those charged with implementing investments (internal or external) specific guidance on growth, income, and timing requirements — but not with detailed instructions as to where the funds should ultimately be invested. The latter, as we will see below, need not be within the province of the board.

There may also be restrictions that apply on an organizationwide basis. Socially or morally based investment criteria, the tax character of an organization (such as a private foundation), or specific legal restrictions on the investments that certain organizations are allowed to make, are all examples of rules that would restrict the investment of organizational funds. Later chapters on the legal environment, portfolio theory, and unique issues facing nonprofits discuss such restrictions and identify methods for addressing them.

ASSESSING TOLERANCE FOR RISK

Perhaps the most important determination that any board must make is: How much risk are the board members willing to assume for each type of fund being invested? A board must make this "gut call" — and must be comfortable with it. Otherwise, losses may cause board members to panic and demand investment strategy changes that disrupt well-laid plans and force hasty, unwise choices.

How should the decision be made? It requires a thoughtful and frank discussion by board members with input from investment advisors and executive staff. The best way I know to accomplish this is to pose a simple, initial question to the members of the board: How much of a loss in this fund in one year (or other period of time) could we tolerate without feeling compelled to change our investment strategy? It is important that the answer be expressed not just in percentage terms, but also in hard dollars. [Too often, I have heard a board member say something like, "A 20 percent drop in our $5 million endowment is acceptable over the next five years." But when I have confirmed this by expressing it in dollar terms — "So it's fine for the endowment to decline by $1 million?" (i.e., 20 percent of $5 million) — the reaction has frequently been "No!"]

Risk tolerance will, and should, vary from fund to fund. But it is vital that a board inform its advisors and executive staff of the level of risk — expressed in dollar terms — that it is willing to accept for each. A professional advisor may also use additional questions, such as those found in Part IV of Appendix V, to help board members determine how much risk they are willing to assume.

Once levels of risk are established, the board's professional advisor can forecast relative risks for the board members and can quantify the likelihood of adverse results. These are not guarantees, of course, but merely guidance.

TIP 1:

Some things cannot be delegated: Only the board can set investment goals and determine its own appetite for risk.

The risk-assessment process should be reiterative. Having once assessed risk tolerance for an organization or for a particular fund, **the board** (or investment committee) **should periodically** (at least annually) **review the assumptions on which risk-tolerance decisions were made.** It may seem odd to suggest that tolerance for risk changes, but that is, in fact, the case. Greater experience, improvement in overall financial strength, or changes in board membership may lead to an increase in risk tolerance. An extended period of poor investment performance or an unanticipated need for immediate spending may provoke a new decision to reduce exposure to risk.

A board of directors has become polarized between board members who wish to increase the return on the organization's $15 million of investable assets and those who want to pursue a much more conservative course of investment. The debate has become acrimonious with the risk-averse board members being called "grannies," who "never made any real money," and the more aggressive colleagues being referred to as "cowboys," who do not appreciate how important it is to preserve the assets of a non-profit. The chair and the chief executive are caught in the middle of this disagreement.

The grannies are advocating placing most funds in long-term government bonds, in an effort at least to out-earn inflation while running little risk of loss of the underly-ing principal. The board chair and chief executive are concerned because they realize that there is a major value risk to the principal, should interest rates rise significantly. On the other hand, the cowboys are advocating heavy investment in equities, though the chair and chief executive are worried about what potential major losses would do to the nonprofit's reputation and to the possibility of future expansion.

How can the volume of the debate be lowered and a consensus reached? The chair and chief executive drew up a list of potential future uses of the investment assets. These included possible program expansion in two years, a capital campaign to pur-chase a headquarters building, and the establishment of an endowment fund. They then asked the board members to divide the investable assets among those potential purposes. This type of discussion tended to be somewhat precise and therefore less emotional.

Then the chief executive and board chair called in the nonprofit's investment advisor and explained to her the purposes of and times at which each fund would be needed. Based on this, she explained to the board the rates of return and levels of risk that would be necessary to achieve each purpose. By asking the board to think about spe-cific objectives for their funds, the chair and chief executive diverted the debate away from an emotional discussion of risk tolerance and toward a more rational discussion of future uses. Having once made those decisions, the board accepted the fairly straightforward risks and returns, as outlined by its professional advisor, that were necessary to carry those decisions to fruition.

CREATING HELPFUL POLICIES AND STRUCTURES

There is an essential difference between *doing* and *supervising*. In the context of this book, the distinction is between selecting specific investments for an organization and supervising (or holding accountable) those who actually do the selecting. My strong belief, based on nearly 25 years in the financial services industry, is that those who supervise should not be the actual investors. To merge the two functions is to effectively eliminate accountability.

But supervision does not imply passivity. There are a number of things that board members must do, or cause to be done, in order to discharge their legal and fiduciary responsibilities — as well as to build a structure that will provide the best opportuni-ty to achieve the board's investment goals. What are the steps a board should take to build a useful structure for investing?

Establish appropriate policies. The first step is to promulgate policies to guide those doing the actual investing. The role of policies is to help everyone remember what the board has decided should be done. In this regard, written investment policies are a must for charitable organizations. They help everyone — board members, executive staff, and outside advisors — understand the organization's investing goals and the risks necessary to achieve those goals. They provide a guiding document that translates organizational objectives into action.

Investment policies also serve another important purpose: limiting organizational liability. Few areas present greater peril to the security and well-being of charitable organizations than the handling of investment assets. It is therefore not surprising that many board members approach investing with hesitation, if not outright reluctance.

But recent laws and legal cases have given a new mandate to board members: discharge or delegate. A board may either discharge its investment responsibilities directly itself or, under the prudent-investor rule (discussed in Chapter 3), delegate its investment responsibilities to others. If board members delegate in an appropriate manner — with sound and clear policy guidance and periodic reviews — they should not be liable for the actions of those to whom they delegate or for investment losses. But if they do so in a careless manner, they retain full responsibility and concomitant liability.

Adopting sound investment policies is one of the actions that a board must take if it is to discharge its fiduciary responsibilities in such a way as to protect both the organization and the individual board members from liability. (A sample set of investment policies is available in Appendix I.)

Hire professional advisors and evaluate their performance. Although the board should not choose specific investments like stocks and bonds, someone has to do it. Delegating this responsibility to someone else is perfectly permissible — if the board is conscientious and careful in its choice. How to go about selecting an advisor and making this most fundamental choice is discussed in Chapter 5.

Hiring an investment advisor is not a one-time event. The board's legal responsibilities are not discharged unless the board (or its investment committee) regularly reviews in a disciplined manner the advisor's work and his or her adherence to the organization's established goals and policies. This is so central to sound investing that any qualified advisor should present a recommended review process as part of the package of services he or she offers. (If he or she does not, place one hand on your wallet and back slowly out of the room!)

Follow-up is an important component of creating the proper structures. It is the continuous process of asking yourself and your advisor if you are doing all the things that you have committed yourselves to do. Performance reporting and evaluation are discussed more thoroughly in the next chapter.

TIP 2:

Structure matters: Adopt a policy, even if it is not perfect, as a first step toward effective investment supervision.

Final Thoughts on the Basics

The good news is that understanding, implementing, and codifying the basics in the form of an investment policy represent a significant portion of everything a board ever needs to do as an investment supervisor.

After that, the board's unique role is to support the organization's staff, members, beneficiaries, and investment advisors by standing by its decisions and giving the basics time to work. This means, among other things, having the courage to stick to your guns during tough times, resisting policy changes that are not thought through carefully because near-term goals are not met, and refusing to allow the occasional downturn in results to cause hurried changes in allocations.

A great benefit of having gone through establishing the basics is that it helps a board resist the passions of the moment. No matter how emotional or fearful we might feel, when we walk into a board meeting and are reminded of well-thought-out policies established after careful reflection, rational decision making becomes *much* easier.

Through the policy-making process, we prepare ourselves and our organizations to facilitate the best in our humanity and to temper our weaknesses. That, ultimately, is the reason to have an investment process that is reflected in investment policies.

Action Questions

1. Have we identified all of our available funds to be invested?

2. Have we secured adequate cash flow for immediate and continuous needs? Do we know what our liquidity needs are?

3. Are we clear about the specific goals and objectives for each of our separate funds?

4. Have we adequately balanced our tolerance for risk with our investment goals?

5. Do we feel well prepared for eventual fluctuations in the money market world?

2.
Investment Concepts for Board Members

There is only a handful of critical investment concepts that every board member should understand:

- the meaning of *total return*

- the use of *portfolio theory* to control risks

- the importance of *time* in managing money

- the role of *performance reporting* as a management tool

TOTAL RETURN

Total return is the entire amount an investment earns, as opposed to just the current income produced (its *yield*). In other words, total return is the sum of dividends, interest, and capital gains, minus any expenses and capital losses. Frequently, the total return on an investment is quite different from the current yield.

By way of example, if you buy a 6 percent bond for $1,000 and hold it for one year, you will receive $60 in interest. But if at the end of the year you sell that bond for $950, your true economic gain would be only $10 ($60 in interest payments reduced by a $50 capital loss). Consequently, the total return on your 6 percent bond would actually be only 1 percent. Measuring an investment on the basis of its total return is the only way to know with any accuracy how well or how poorly an investment is performing.

In the investment world, total return is usually measured annually on a calendar basis for individual investors, and on a trailing, quarterly basis for institutional accounts. To compute total return, the amount of capital gain or loss is determined by assuming that the investment was purchased on the first day of the year (or period in question) and sold on the last. To this capital gain or loss the total of all dividend or interest payments received for the period in question is added, with any expenses incurred (such as trading costs) subtracted. Results are often reported both before and after investment management fees, if any.

One frequent objection to this way of measuring total return is that it treats unrealized gains and losses as if they were realized (i.e., as if the investment had been sold and an actual gain or loss realized). Intuitively, an unrealized loss should not be as bad as a realized loss since there is still the possibility that the unsold investment will regain its value.

Why, for example, should it matter if a bond has decreased in value if the investor intends to hold it to maturity? It matters a great deal because the loss is real whether you are forced to realize it or not. At that particular moment, the organization has fewer assets on its books and less money available for its charitable purposes, no matter how certain the future appreciation may seem. In addition, there is an *opportunity cost* inherent in each investment. Continuing to hold an investment is essentially the same as deciding to buy that instrument instead of another. (This is particularly true in highly liquid markets with low commission costs.) In reality, if the organization wishes to switch to another investment, it can only do so with the reduced amount.

Annual total returns, as reported by all reputable investment advisors and as shown in most published indices, include both realized and unrealized gains and losses. A major benefit of this approach is that it recognizes that there is almost always a possibility of the investor being forced to sell an investment. It also highlights losses much sooner than would be the case by other measurements. Nonprofit accounting conventions now require the recognition of unrealized gains and losses in a nonprofit's financial records. In this regard, the accounting profession agrees with the investment community on the most accurate method of measuring total return. Any nonprofit board will want to understand this concept and measure its own investment performance by total return.

PORTFOLIO THEORY TO CONTROL RISK

At its most basic, risk is the possibility of a bad result. More technically, it is the measurable possibility of an investment losing, as opposed to gaining, value. There are numerous sources of risk. They include

- *individual-investment risk:* the risk associated with the decline in value of any one stock or bond, which is also called *specific risk*

- *market risk:* the risk that all stocks and bonds in a particular market will decline in value

- *liquidity risk:* the possibility that market conditions preclude selling an asset

- *interest-rate risk:* the risk that changes in interest rates will cause capital losses in interest-rate sensitive investments, such as bonds or preferred stock

- *inflation risk:* the risk that inflation will erode the purchasing power and therefore the true value of an investment return

- *currency risk:* the possibility that an investment denominated in a currency other than the U.S. dollar will decline in value when converted back into dollars, due to a decrease in the value of the currency relative to the dollar

Current thinking about controlling risk is based on *portfolio theory*. The essence of the theory is that portfolios, which are simply a collection of assets, can be created in optimal ways so that an investor can, to some extent, reduce the amount of risk he or she is taking for a given level of anticipated return. The risk of illiquidity, for example, can be virtually eliminated by confining a portfolio's investments to major markets.

In recent years, an enormous amount of literature from the professional and academic investment communities has focused on risk. As a result, understanding of the risk-return relationship is improving. We have long known, for example, that there is a correlation between the amount of risk an investor assumes and the anticipated return: The greater an investment's inherent risk, the greater the anticipated return a rational investor will demand for taking this risk.

As a result of modern studies, we also know that investors are rewarded with greater returns for taking some risks but not others. The risks for which there is a corresponding reward are generally those, such as market risk, that cannot be avoided. There is not, on the other hand, a reward for taking *avoidable* risks, such as the risk of being undiversified.

There are two major techniques in portfolio theory to reduce risk:

1. **Diversification** is the distribution of investment funds among different instruments (typically stocks and/or bonds) for the purpose of reducing the *specific risk* associated with any one investment. A number of studies have shown that when a portfolio is diversified over 18 to 20 equity investments, more than 90 percent of specific risk is eliminated. In other words, having that many different securities in a portfolio will effectively eliminate the risk that any one stock can significantly diminish the portfolio's value.

2. **Asset allocation** is the distribution of investment funds among different classes of assets, such as stocks, bonds, foreign investments, and cash. **It can be thought of as diversification on a grand scale.** The theory underlying asset allocation is that asset classes will tend to react differently to the same outside economic events (referred to as *noncorrelation*). When investment managers refer to asset allocation, they mean the process of investing in different asset classes in order to reduce overall risk for a given level of anticipated return.

   To use a simple example, if stocks go up when bonds go down, then a portfolio consisting of stocks and bonds should have less risk than an all-stock portfolio. The same difference in response to economic events that occurs between stocks and bonds also occurs between U.S. stocks and foreign stocks, or between U.S. stocks and cash investments. By focusing on the ways that classes of assets behave, investors can attempt to take the least amount of risk for a given level of projected return.

But effective diversification requires more than just having 20 different stocks in a portfolio. The equities must also be in companies in different lines of business — because stocks of similar companies (which is to say, those in the same industry or sector) tend to respond in the same way to external economic events. A portfolio of 20 electric-utility stocks or one of 20 airline stocks would not be adequately diversified to reduce risk. In both cases, the stocks, as a group, would tend to behave similarly in response to changes in interest rates, to increases in oil prices, or to other outside economic events. *Sector* diversification — being invested in different industry groups or sectors — is crucial to reducing risk.

The lack of sector diversification explains why those who invested so heavily in high-flying dot-com or telecommunication stocks in the late 1990s were so badly hurt: They were concentrating their investments in narrowly focused stocks, mutual funds, or fund managers. When the limits of Internet profit potential, the overbuilding of fiber-optic networks, and the costs to telecoms of deregulation became apparent, the shares of all companies in that particular sector declined. In that situation, owning 20 or more different companies provided inadequate diversification.

Combined together, asset allocation among classes of assets, and diversification of stocks and bonds among different industries and sectors are potent tools for reducing risk in an organization's portfolio of investments.

THE IMPORTANCE OF TIME IN MANAGING MONEY

Time often cures a multitude of sins. And this is nowhere more evident than in the investment world. Those with patience are usually rewarded: There has been only one 15-year period since World War II during which the stock market lost money, and there are no 20-year periods. History tells us that — even without the benefit of professional management or of risk-reducing asset allocations — a 100 percent investment in the stock market will eventually make money, if given enough time.

This means that for endowments and other long-term funds with allocations to the equity markets, the longer the time frame the better. Unfortunately, our natural tendency is to think more short-term than is actually reasonable: In the institutional investment world, of which nonprofits are a part, consultants and investment committees commonly review a manager's performance quarterly. This is a good discipline. But equity portfolio managers as a group have very little control over quarterly returns. If they make good investments, the value of the portfolio will increase ... *over time*. But it will not increase *every quarter* and the dips and bumps are largely unpredictable.

For a board of directors and their investment committee, it is important to establish a relationship between the time frames applied to a particular portfolio and the board's risk tolerance. With endowments and other permanent funds, we may decide that three-year rolling numbers will be the primary measure of our portfolio's investment performance. Since those funds have a perpetual investment horizon, why get overly concerned with near-term numbers? But to take that approach, we need to understand how much our portfolio might decline in any three-year period **and then we need to be comfortable with that level of risk.** While intermediate term volatility really *should* not matter, if we cannot sleep at night because of the declines in our portfolios, we will not be able to maintain our allocations and thereby obtain the benefits of long-term investing.

TIP 3:

Determine specific criteria for knowing when to change your regular investment committee meeting to an emergency meeting in order to avoid becoming too reactive to market fluctuations.

PERFORMANCE REPORTING AS AN INVESTMENT MANAGEMENT TOOL

Performance reports measure the change in value of an investment for a given period. Their purpose is to provide a reasonable and informed view of how well (or how poorly) an organization's investments are doing. The best reports will also give us some idea of how much risk we have taken to achieve the results. Consequently, board members, and especially members of an investment committee, will typically want to spend significant time understanding and interpreting these reports. The committee's review of performance reports is an essential component of overall investment success.

It should be emphasized here that performance reporting is quite different from financial accounting. The latter is intended to convey an accurate reflection of organizational value at a given point in time. It is easy to confuse the two. In addition, it is important to distinguish between custodial statements and performance reports.

1. **Custodial:** A custodial statement is a report, usually issued monthly, by the legal entity (e.g., bank, brokerage house, trust company) that has custody of another's assets. It reflects all of the investments in an account with month-end values. It also includes unrealized gains and losses on all investments and itemizes all transactions that occurred during the period, including purchases and sales, additions or withdrawals of funds, and the payment of any expenses.

   The purpose of custodial reports is to verify the existence of the organization's assets with a statement that can be reconciled to internal records. This represents the absolute minimum information that an organization should receive. To adequately discharge their supervisory duty, board members must also have reports that provide essential third-party information and historical data that custodial reports do not include.

2. **Performance:** A performance report focuses on changes in the value of an investment account for a given period. In addition, such reports typically *measure* those changes against appropriate indices and, sometimes, against competing investment providers. More elaborate reports may also provide assessments of performance relative to risk. The most elaborate reports analyze performance through multiple statistical measures in an attempt to identify the sources of success or failure.

Performance reports are typically provided quarterly. They usually show performance for the most recent quarter, as well as for the most recent calendar year, trailing year, or both. As longer histories of an organization's investments become available, they will typically report on longer trailing periods such as three, five, and 10 years. Most reports use easy-to-understand graphs and color.

There is a wide variety of standard indices against which the performance of a portfolio can be measured. There are narrow indices, such as the Dow Jones Industrial Average of 30 stocks, and broad indices, such as the Wilshire 5000, which is a weighted-average index of most publicly traded stocks in the United States for which price quotes are available. There are also "style" indices for specific equity categories such as value, growth, and small capitalization stocks, as well as numerous fixed-income and international indices.

It is important that you and your advisor choose an appropriate index, or blend of indices, against which to measure each of the organization's funds. Otherwise, you may be comparing apples to oranges. It would be misleading, for example, to compare a 50 percent equity and 50 percent bond portfolio to the S&P500, which is an all-stock index. Most of the time, such a comparison will not tell you whether your investments — and your investment advisor — are doing well ... only that stocks outperformed bonds, or vice versa.

Because performance reporting can be somewhat complex, most board members will benefit from spending some time with their investment advisor in order to obtain a full understanding of the reports. An advisor's guidance will be invaluable, for this is one area in which the time you spend developing greater knowledge will certainly pay off — for you and your organization.

ACTION QUESTIONS

1. When assessing the success of our investments, are we relying on correct data on which to base our judgment?

2. Are we protecting our assets via adequate asset allocation and diversification?

3. Do we receive relevant reports that allow us to assess true performance of our investments?

3.
The Legal Environment

For well over a century, the operative rule governing investments by fiduciaries was the so-called *prudent-man rule*. In the last 30 years, however, the prudent-*man* rule has largely been replaced by the prudent-*investor* rule. While this may sound like a politically correct name change, it is in fact a substantive legal change, which, with a few exceptions, is now the law of the land.

In this chapter, the following items will be explored:

- the background to rules on prudent investing for nonprofits

- today's legal environment: the prudent-investor rule

- standard of care and delegation of authority

- restraints on the prudent-investor rule

BACKGROUND: THE PRUDENT-MAN RULE

The prudent-man rule traces its roots to the 1830 case of *Harvard College v. Amory* in the Supreme Judicial Court of Massachusetts. In that case, the judge wrote that, when investing, a trustee of funds

> … is to observe how men of prudence, discretion, and intelligence manage their own affairs, not in regard to speculation, but in regard to the permanent disposition of their funds, considering the probable income, as well as the probable safety of the capital to be invested.

The prudent-man rule sounded reasonable and accommodating, but as it evolved, it became narrower and more restrictive. As states began to codify the prudent-man rule, their legislatures often went much further in restricting investments by fiduciaries. Some laws actually specified lists of acceptable investments and became known as *legal list* statutes. Others restricted fiduciaries to investing in U.S. government securities and high-grade corporate bonds. Ownership of common stocks was often prohibited.

Judicial interpretation of the prudent-man rule also tended toward cautious and conservative results. Nothing became more important than the preservation of capital. The board members' primary responsibility was to never lose money on the underlying investment. In addition, investments were expected to generate current income, which made non–income producing assets suspect, if not outright inappropriate.

Most importantly, in determining prudence each investment was judged independently and not as part of a collection or portfolio of investments. Board members could be liable for losses incurred on a single investment, even if the overall performance of the portfolio was excellent. Overall, the laws and the courts' interpretations of them encouraged fiduciaries to adopt extremely conservative investment attitudes, usually entirely excluding any investment in common stocks.

The attitudes created during the primacy of the prudent-man rule still linger in the nonprofit community. An occasional organization, for example, still invests endowment and other longer-term funds in certificates of deposit and U.S. government bonds. But that is an increasingly rare event. As the new rules described below have now been in place in most states for anywhere from 10 to 30 years, the issue today is how to live with the investment freedom that flows from those rules. As we shall see, the law of prudent investing now permits board members and other fiduciaries to utilize virtually any investment vehicle available.

THE PRUDENT-INVESTOR RULE

The catalysts for change were the high inflation of the late 1960s and early 1970s, and the development of risk-reducing portfolio theory.

When inflation exceeded an unprecedented 13 percent in the late 1970s, holders of low-risk but fixed-income portfolios found themselves hemorrhaging money. Essentially, they were lending dollars and being repaid in dimes. As they saw their assets rapidly dwindling, many trustees and beneficiaries began questioning the constrictions of the prudent-man rule.

At the same time, portfolio theory to reduce risk was moving out of academia and into practical application. The two trends — high inflation and modern portfolio theory — resulted in a notable 1969 Ford Foundation study entitled "The Law and the Lore of Endowment Funds." That study, and a companion study five years later, collectively recommended creating clear rules that would allow universities (and by extension, all nonprofits) to "spend" principal and to invest for total return. These studies, and the publicity surrounding them, led directly to the widespread adoption of the prudent-investor rule.

There are two primary statutory expressions of the prudent-investor rule. The Uniform Management of Institutional Funds Act (UMIFA) first promulgated in 1972. UMIFA applies broadly to any "incorporated or unincorporated organization organized and operated exclusively for educational, religious, charitable, or other eleemosynary purposes...." It is currently enacted in the vast majority of the states and the District of Columbia (please see Appendix III). In 1994, the National Conference of Commissioners on Uniform State Laws promulgated the Uniform Prudent Investor Act (UPIA), which applies these same concepts to trusts and is also in force in most states (see Appendix IV).

UMIFA §1(1) and the Uniform Prudent Investor Act both apply to charitable trusts; therefore, in most states, the funds of the organization itself — and any funds for which a charitable nonprofit serves as trustee, such as charitable-remainder trusts — are governed by the same prudent-investor standards.

Even in the few states that have not adopted these uniform laws, the concepts embodied in them are usually applicable. In 1990, the American Law Institute issued a restatement of the investment-standards portion of the Law of Trusts, which incorporated prudent-investor concepts. (The Law of Trusts is a "common law" guide to attorneys and judges in states without those statutes.)

The discussion below focuses primarily on UMIFA because that statute applies most directly to the management of nonprofit funds. However, UPIA, as a more recent expression of the prudent-investor rule, is also referred to below.

STANDARD OF CARE

Under both acts, the definition of prudence focuses on investment processes as opposed to classifying a specific investment or a course of action as prudent or imprudent. The standard-of-care language in UMIFA protects board members from hindsight and second-guessing by providing that "a governing board shall exercise ordinary business care and prudence *under the facts and circumstances prevailing at the time of the action or decision.*"[2] [Emphasis added.]

A nonprofit board of directors is instructed to

> ... consider long and short term needs of the institution in carrying out its educational, religious, charitable, or other eleemosynary purposes, its present and anticipated financial requirements, expected total return on its investments, price level trends, and general economic conditions.[3]

Collectively, this language permits fiduciaries to include in a portfolio a reasonable proportion of higher-risk investments, without fear of being held liable after the fact for the losses on any single investment. (UPIA is even more explicit: "A trustee's investment and management decisions respecting individual assets must be evaluated not in isolation but in the context of the trust portfolio as a whole and as part of an overall investment strategy having risk and return objectives reasonably suited to the trust."[4]) The language also places capital gains on an equal footing with dividends and income.

Inherent in this portfolio approach is a diversification requirement, which is implied in UMIFA and explicit in UPIA and in other state statutes. The law takes an extremely dim view of nondiversified investments unless such lack of diversification is either mandated by a trust instrument or is essential to the purposes of the organization.

Nonprofits are also, for the first time, specifically authorized to take into consideration their "educational, religious, charitable, or other eleemosynary purposes." Organizations with strong social, political, moral, or religious doctrines may eschew investments they believe are philosophically incompatible with their purpose — and they may do so even if the result is a lower total return.

Finally, in evaluating anticipated returns, the laws specifically acknowledge the importance of protecting assets from the effects of inflation. Section 6 of UMIFA provides that the board is to consider both "the long and short term needs of the institution," as well as "price trends and general economic conditions."

2. UMIFA §6
3. UMIFA §6
4. UPIA §2 (b)

DELEGATION OF AUTHORITY

Another significant change embodied in the prudent-investor rule is the ability of board members to delegate investment authority. The power to delegate is a reflection of the tremendous complexity associated with modern investing. Not only may the board "delegate to committees, officers, or employees of the institution or the fund," but it may also "contract with independent investment advisers, investment counsel or managers, banks, or trust companies...."[5]

UPIA also specifically authorizes a trust's directors to delegate investment and management functions. A trustee is no longer liable to the beneficiaries of the trust for the decisions or actions of the agent. In other words, a charitable board may delegate management of its planned-gift trusts to an outside investment manager and thereby relieve the organization of liability for the investment decisions.

To be shielded from liability, a board must use reasonable care and skill in (1) selecting the advisor, (2) directing the advisor, and (3) reviewing the advisor's performance. To adequately direct an advisor, a nonprofit must adopt and convey to that advisor its investment policy decisions. Therefore, the existence of appropriate policies is a prerequisite to limiting the organization's and the board's liability.

CASE STUDY: APPROPRIATE DELEGATION

The new chief executive of a midsized nonprofit has had a considerable amount of investment experience, both personally and in previous jobs at other nonprofits. He has a more extensive and sophisticated knowledge of investment than any current board member. He has offered to relieve the board members of the burden of supervision of their investment advisor, to perform the work of the board's investment committee, and to report to the board at its semiannual meetings.

What concerns are raised by this proposal to delegate its authority to the chief executive?
First, no matter how capable the chief executive, the board is ultimately responsible for the investment decisions — by law and custom. Therefore a meaningful level of review of the chief executive's activities and decisions on investing is required. Is that satisfied by a semiannual report by the chief executive to the board? The board members decide, quite rightly, that it is not.

Are more heads better than one?
The board members also felt that regular participation by some of them on an investment committee — even if they were less knowledgeable than the chief executive — would bring more balance, common sense, and thoughtfulness to decision making than one very busy chief executive acting alone.

Finally, the board decided that is was wrong to ask their chief executive to properly judge the risk tolerance of the board and to make the other basic decisions on which investments would be made, if it was not sufficiently engaged in the process. Rather than abdicating all these responsibilities, the board voted to retain its investment committee — but added the chief executive to its membership.

---

5. UMIFA §5

RESTRAINTS ON THE UNIFORM ACTS

You might infer from this brief discussion of prudent-investor rules that nothing is prohibited outright — that virtually any investment is available to nonprofits. Investment prudence is to be judged in the aggregate, not one investment at a time. Therefore, common stocks of all types (large, small, domestic, and foreign), private placements, hedge funds, and other derivatives are all fair game. Managing investments in a world of greater choice is the new challenge.

But there are important exceptions to this general rule as a result of either (a) the incomplete adoption of prudent-investor concepts, or (b) the existence of special rules (usually tax-related) that apply to certain organizations or in certain circumstances.

First, the so-called *uniform acts* are legislative proposals recommended to the states for enactment by a drafting commission. While most states have adopted these proposals, not all have and not all have adopted the acts in their entirety or without important changes. (The legislature of my home state of California almost always makes changes in the proposed language when adopting a uniform act.) Therefore, it is vital to learn from your legal counsel exactly what laws and concepts apply in your state.

Second, the old prudent-man concept was embedded in jurisprudence for so many years that it still lies tucked away in unsuspected corners of statutes in many states. For example, gift-annuity reserves in some states are still governed by anachronistic prudent-man concepts. Again, advice of counsel is the best way to keep from being blind-sided by a prudent-man provision.

Some tax laws, federal and state, place restrictions — explicit and implicit — on nonprofits. In 1969, for example, Congress adopted new tax rules for private foundations, charitable-remainder trusts, and charitable-lead trusts. Those rules contain a handful of investment restrictions. Private foundations, for example, are not allowed to make *jeopardy investments*. The term applies to investments that are so inherently risky that they might jeopardize the viability of the organization. Unfortunately, the term jeopardy investment is not clearly-defined in either the code or the regulations so there is an understandable hesitancy on the part of private foundations to criticize some of the more esoteric modern investment instruments.

THE CONSTRAINT OF BROADER FIDUCIARY DUTY

While UMIFA and UPIA impose specific guidance for directors and trustees, general, common-law duties also arise out of trust relationships, either express or implied.

As stated in the past, "A fiduciary is a person or an entity who holds a trust relationship to another. Anyone who controls assets or exercises power or authority for the benefit of someone else is said to be a 'fiduciary,' and such a person's responsibilities are referred to as 'fiduciary duties.' It is a very broad concept with deep roots in Anglo-American law."[6] If a nonprofit organization serves as trustee for a charitable trust, for example, that organization as a trustee owes a fiduciary duty to the beneficiaries, who are those people or entities for whose benefit the trust exists.

---

6. Fry, Robert P. Jr. *Nonprofit Investment Polices: Practical Steps for Growing Charitable Funds.* New York: John Wiley & Sons, 1998.

Fiduciary duty is an even broader concept in the nonprofit world because, in most states, such duty is an express part of the laws governing nonprofit organizations. Specifically, nonprofits are deemed to be holding all of their assets, including investment funds, in trust for the benefit of the constituencies and the charitable purposes for which the organization exists. The state attorney general is typically given broad authority to enforce the trust concept and to prevent the theft, misuse, or mismanagement of a nonprofit organization's funds.

The concept of fiduciary duty infuses all aspects of nonprofit investment management, as a complement to specific investment laws like UMIFA. In practice, it means that, even if a particular investment is appropriate under prudent-investor concepts, that investment still might not be appropriate under fiduciary concepts, if, for example, it creates a conflict of interest. Fiduciary duty is the ultimate constraint on what is otherwise a very liberal, modern investment environment created by the prudent-investor rule.

ACTION QUESTIONS

1. Do we understand the changes between the prudent-man rule and prudent-investor rule and how the differences affect our investment flexibility?

2. Have we protected ourselves from liability by delegating the investment authority to a qualified outside expert?

3. Does our investment committee understand its fiduciary role?

4.
Unique Issues Facing Nonprofits

Nonprofit organizations can benefit from investment theory, methods, and practices developed by the for-profit world. But there are significant differences and restraints on charitable organizations and, because these differences often relate to investment policies and practices by charities, it is important that they are understood by nonprofit boards. These important differences include the following:

- the types of funds under management

- the role of an investment committee

- the interaction between investment policy and donors

- spending policy

- conflicts of interest

TYPES OF FUNDS

At the start, it should be clear that this discussion is not about fund accounting. That is an accounting concept by which nonprofits track their funds and under which they are required to categorize their funds as *unrestricted, temporarily restricted,* or *permanently restricted.* These categories are intended to describe an organization's *access* to the funds, not to tell you *how* the various funds in question should be invested.

Much more pertinent for investment purposes is categorizing funds as to *when they need to be accessed* by a nonprofit. Funds can be divided into two broad categories: operating reserves and long-term assets. *Operating reserves* include any funds being held for general spending within the next 12 months. *Long-term funds* always include permanent endowments — funds from which the organization may only spend a limited amount in order to ensure the fund's perpetual existence — and may also include retirement assets, gift-annuity reserves, or other funds with a long-term purpose and time horizon.

Beyond the types of funds described above, the board is free to exercise its judgment in categorizing other money of the nonprofit. Many charities raise money in capital campaigns, the goal of which is to renovate or purchase new facilities. But often there is a long period of time — sometimes many years — in which the funds could be invested before being spent. How such funds should be invested is tied directly to the time available for investment.

The time available is usually the single-most important factor that determines how a fund may or should be invested. Short-term funds (those that might be spent within 12 months) generally should be kept in cash or cash equivalents, such as money market funds. Intermediate-term funds (those expected to be available in one to five years) may be invested in fixed-income instruments, such as corporate or government bonds, in maturities that are appropriate for the length of time the funds are available.

Longer-term funds (those that will be available for five years or more) can be invested in equities and other comparable investments.

THE ROLE OF AN INVESTMENT COMMITTEE

In any corporation, nonprofit or otherwise, ultimate responsibility for the health and well-being of the entity rests with the board of directors. But as a practical matter, most boards delegate the actual authority over more complex operations to committees or to its executive staff. This is often the case with investments. An investment committee is, typically, a smaller committee of board members that may also include additional nondirectors as committee members. While there are many variations of how investment committees are established, it is not uncommon for the nonprofit's chief financial officer to chair the committee and to act as a conduit between the committee and those delegated to do the actual work.

Under most state corporation laws, a board can delegate its authority to properly constituted committees. Therefore, an investment committee can largely serve in the board's place in supervising the investment process. This allows investment supervision to be exercised by those board members who have the time, interest, and knowledge that such supervision requires.

The committee's role is to supervise those who are actually doing the investing, whether they are internal executives, outside consultants and managers, or both. (A few nonprofits with large investments may be able to bring some functions in-house, but it is still important to maintain an independent supervisory infrastructure.) The committee should carefully review the regular and periodic performance reports submitted by its staff and outside advisors. Typically, such reviews occur quarterly with a face-to-face annual meeting. Beyond this, how active the committee might be will depend on the size of the organization, the complexity of the investments, and the presence or absence of internal staff available to assist.

Remember that, under prudent-investor laws, for an investment committee to do an adequate job of delegation (and to shield it and the board from liability), the committee must use reasonable care and skill in (1) selecting an advisor, (2) directing the advisor, and (3) reviewing the advisor's performance.

Should board members ever choose specific investments themselves? Nonprofit board members generally should not actively manage the organization's own investments. The board members' role is to supervise those who are actually doing the investing, whether they are internal staff or external advisors. Direct investing by board members usually means that no one is effectively supervising those who are doing the investing work. Additionally, choosing the right investments is a difficult job requiring the knowledge, experience, and discipline of a professional. Few board members can bring that to the table.

INTERACTION BETWEEN INVESTMENT POLICY AND DONORS

Nonprofits are different from for-profit companies in their dependence on and relationships with donors and other constituents. Frequently, an organization's donors are partners in the work and mission of the organization, giving of themselves as volunteers and supporting the organization in many other ways (besides just writing checks). Understanding how investment policies may impact donors, and vice versa, is important for a nonprofit board.

GIVING DONORS CONFIDENCE

Whether a donor contributes $5 or $5 million, he or she is entrusting his or her gift to a nonprofit in the belief that the funds will be used well and wisely by the board to accomplish the nonprofit's mission or ministry. To the extent that a nonprofit has a surplus or maintains an endowment, having an investment policy in place is one of the most important things a board can do to give donors confidence in the soundness of a nonprofit's management, and to reassure donors that their trust will not be betrayed through sloppiness or neglect by the board. A sound investment policy and process serves donors by making the organization worthy of a gift.

GIFT-ACCEPTANCE POLICIES

Most assets of a nonprofit start out as gifts. If the gift is cash, no particular issues are raised beyond proper accounting and record keeping. But what about gifts of publicly traded stock?

Tax law provides strong incentives to donors to give gifts of appreciated stock directly, instead of selling the stock and donating the cash value. For gifts of appreciated publicly traded stock, the donor receives an income-tax charitable deduction for the full fair market value of the gifted shares without having to pay any tax on the embedded capital gains. From a tax perspective, that is a powerful inducement to many donors.

Consequently, gifts of appreciated stock are becoming more frequent. How, then, should a nonprofit handle these gifts? Stock gifts should be delivered to the organization's investment advisors for immediate evaluation. The only question the advisor needs to answer is: Would the nonprofit normally hold such a position in its portfolio? If the answer is "no," the stock should be sold, as the only cost of doing so will be the relatively minor sales charges, if any.

To do otherwise (e.g., to keep shares simply because they were donated to the nonprofit) is essentially to abandon investment discipline. A large gift of stock to a small organization, for example, can skew the portfolio toward a particular sector or industry. It can also result in inadequate diversification that puts the nonprofit's investments at greater risk. Whatever the impact may be, it is almost certain that it will not be an investment anticipated by the organization's investment strategy.

Wealthy donors often have a high opinion of their own investment knowledge. By having both investment and gift acceptance policies in place ahead of time, it is much easier to inform major donors of the intended disposition of their gift of shares — without having that action seem personal or critical.

GIFTS OF OTHER HARD ASSETS

Sometimes a donor will want to contribute an asset other than stocks or bonds. These gifts might include *hard* assets, such as real estate, art, or jewelry; or *intangible* assets, such as mineral interests, closely held stock, or intellectual property. Such gifts are more difficult to handle than publicly traded stocks and bonds because they are often highly illiquid.

Before accepting such a gift, a nonprofit should secure a professional evaluation of the gift that would include valuation, marketability, storage and insurance costs, and other potential liabilities, such as environmental. (An environmental liability can sometimes exceed the value of a piece of real estate!)

Most gifts of this kind, if accepted, should be sold immediately and not held as an investment, unless there is a specific mission or ministry reason for doing so (e.g., the gift of a building appropriate for the organization's use.)

SOCIALLY RESPONSIBLE INVESTING

Over the past decade, a growing number of nonprofits have included "socially responsible" guidelines in their investment policies. The most popular approach is portfolio screening. Many nonprofits attempt to "screen" their investments to eliminate those that are inconsistent with their missions. For many organizations, it is important to make this effort. The most common companies avoided are those involved in tobacco, alcohol, gambling, pornography, and weapons production.

Within reasonable limits, screening based on social and moral criteria is usually feasible. Advisors can accommodate social screens in individually managed accounts and either maintain restricted lists internally or outsource that work to social research firms. So long as we understand the limitations, this can be a worthy effort.

One limitation is the sheer complexity of capital markets in our now global economy. Even with computerized databases and vast quantities of research, it is still a daunting task to ferret out all the activities of major corporations. Additionally, screening is virtually impossible through index funds and most mainstream mutual funds because of their broad holdings (although there are some socially responsible mutual funds).

Finally, I have yet to see a nonprofit investment policy that prohibits holding U.S. government securities (usually the essential core of a fixed-income portfolio). Yet any organization that owns federal bonds but which is concerned about alcohol, tobacco, gambling, nuclear energy, or armaments, is "investing" in each of those activities since the federal government is either an active participant or a silent partner in all.

A reasonable approach to screening is to inform your advisors of the sectors, industries, or specific companies that your organization would like to avoid. So long as the list is not excessive, your advisors should be able to honor such requests.

Nonprofits have also become active in a second approach to socially responsible investing: shareholder advocacy. As shareowners of publicly traded companies, nonprofits have discovered a voice and vote through the annual proxy statement. They have learned that they can use their investments, as well as their programs, to effect positive change in the global economy, environment, and culture. In 2003, several hundred shareholder resolutions were filed, addressing corporate behaviors ranging from executive compensation to disclosure of environmental impacts. Several nonprofits have established proxy-voting guidelines that direct how their shares should be voted and that are executed by outside firms. Many have found that the time and expense of developing and implementing proxy-voting guidelines is an effective strategy to promote their missions.

For some nonprofits, another effective approach to socially responsible investing may be available: direct investment in for-profit companies working to correct a social ill or conducting business in a manner that is consistent with the nonprofit's mission. Investments of this type have been made over the years, largely by grantmaking foundations, under the name of program-related investments (PRIs). In recent years, some donors, instead of simply donating money, have turned their entrepreneurial energies to helping nonprofits invest in their missions. At times, entirely new for-profit organizations have been developed to support such efforts. The result of these investments can be excellent for both donor and organization. For the donor, a far higher level of personal participation, commitment, and satisfaction may result. For the organization, a new, continuing, and secure source of funding is developed.

But many nonprofit missions cannot, in fact, be supported in a profit-making manner. By their very natures, nonprofit missions usually exist to fill a service gap that is not being met by for-profit businesses (because there is no "profit" in the service) or by the government (because there is no political will or funding for the service). Nonprofits serving the poorest and weakest people in society fall into that category.

Another example is *pure* or *primary* medical research that is decades away from practical application or any sort of economic return. In many cases, therefore, neither for-profit endeavors nor PRIs will be a substitute for old-fashioned fundraising.

Nevertheless, nonprofit boards should be open, when it is feasible, to the possibility of PRIs. Perhaps the best way to approach such an investment is to set aside some portion of a nonprofit's assets for investment in a for-profit, mission-motivated venture. A board could deliberately set aside a portion of the nonprofit's endowment or other reserve for this purpose — but only if such funds could be lost in their entirety without endangering the life or work of the organization. The balance of the nonprofit's fund could then be invested in accordance with the board's regular investment policies. By taking this approach, a board may avoid the temptation to take inappropriate PRI risks for the sake of its mission or ministry.

SCAM-PROOFING

Another way to build donor confidence and giving is for the board to ensure that an organization's invested assets are protected from fraud and other chicanery.

Putting sound investment policies in place is the best thing a board can do to scam-proof an organization. Beyond that there are two other keys for the board. First, every financial transaction must be classified as either an investment or a gift. Here is the difference: If you expect to receive your funds back, it is an investment. If not, it is a gift. Once the board has identified the intended transaction as an investment, the application of normal investment policies and procedures should be sufficient to avoid most scams.

Second, a board is in the best position to create an organizational atmosphere of patience and caution. The fundraising world is a tough one and there are scam artists and smooth talkers in it (as well as some legitimate and dedicated people). The pressure on nonprofit executives and staff may make them vulnerable to ventures that are questionable or have little real chance of successful payback. The board should build an organizational culture of caution, beginning with a board declaration that the directors bear the ultimate responsibility for the financial health of the organization and are there to assist the executives and staff in the onerous job of raising the funds to support the vital work of their nonprofit.

SPENDING POLICY

Operating reserves (short-term money) are there to be spent as the board members best determine. But the board needs to decide how much of its permanent funds should be used for current spending. Deciding how much to spend and what the sources to support spending ought to be frequently become the tail that wags the board's investment dog.

In the old prudent-man world, it was generally acceptable to "spend the income." Dividends and interest could be spent, but capital gains needed to be retained. Thus, the only ways to increase spending were either to increase the yield on fixed-income investments or to shift assets away from low- or non-dividend-paying investments in favor of better yield-generating ones.

With the advent of the prudent-investor concept and its emphasis on investing for total return, there is now less need to restrict spending to income from a strictly legal perspective. (There may still be circumstances in which spending is constrained by the terms of a specific instrument or other legal requirement, but when that is not the case, spending policy should be based on total return.)

Colleges and universities have led the way in developing a widely used model for spending long-term funds. While details vary, a common policy is to spend 5 percent of net asset value in quarterly increments on a 36-month or 12-trailing-quarter basis. A number of academic studies have indicated that spending in excess of 5 percent is not sustainable over the long run.

What this policy produces is a steady and predictable spending pattern that is the natural result of averaging net asset values over a trailing three-year period as the basis of the amount to be spent. Therefore, large capital gains in one quarter will only increase spending slightly, just as major losses will only lower it slightly. [Because markets have trended upward over long periods of time, a spending policy based on trailing values will also tend to lower the amount to be spent. Thus, a 5 percent policy, as calculated above, will turn out, in practice, to produce a slightly lower amount (such as 4.75 percent of the current values)].

There are several significant advantages to this model: First, it effectively isolates investment policy from spending pressures. Spending will come in a disciplined and predetermined way from all available assets and will not be dependent solely on income. Therefore, investment policy can be established based on overall risk-and-return objectives without having to artificially allocate investment funds to bonds or other fixed-income instruments for the sole purpose of generating income.

Secondly, such a policy makes spending highly predictable. An organization's treasurer, controller, or chief financial officer can make a reasonable estimate of actual spending at the beginning of each year. Even large capital gains or large losses will not have a major impact on budgets and spending.

The final benefit of such an approach is that it will often eliminate contentious discussion about spending at the board level. If investment returns are strong, spending will increase — but slowly — and the fund will grow as a result of the excess. If losses are incurred, spending will be reduced, but slowly. The organization is thereby insulated from wild swings in spending — and painful decisions having to be made by the board.

TIP 4:

Determine your spending policy before determining what you need to earn. Remember that if you set your spending rate at 5 percent and the inflation is 3 percent, you must get a return of 8 percent, net of all expenses.

CASE STUDY: SPENDING VS. INVESTING

A nonprofit with substantial investments has been spending on programs 5 percent of its invested assets for the last five years. About 25 percent of the investment funds have been restricted by the donor as an endowment for which the corpus may not be spent. Because of a conservative investment strategy, the underlying value of the investments has been relatively unscathed by the market fluctuations since 2000. This year, because of greater demand on the organization's programs, some members of the board advocated increasing the amount of spending from 5 to 8 or 10 percent per year. How did the board go about deciding on this question?

The first issue the board examined was the program needs that were being used to justify an increase in spending. Were they legitimate? Were they immediate? Or could they be postponed or spread out over several years to minimize the financial impact? Were there other ways to pay for the program increases, such as other funding sources, partnering with another organization, or a fee-for-service program?

Ultimately, the board determined that the increased program spending was justified and that there were no funding sources other than assets. They then faced a quandary: how to increase spending from assets without invading the principal of the restricted endowment fund.

Several board members argued for a more aggressive investment strategy that would produce higher returns from which to fund increased programs. Their investment advisor cautioned, however, that this was not a good strategy to follow for the short term. Quick gains in the equity or bond markets — to fund the program increases — would be a most risky and uncertain gamble.

Other board members advocated invading the corpus of the restricted endowment, since the law in their state permitted some limited spending of the principal. However, the board determined that it should honor the original intentions of the donor.

Another board member stated that, with a less conservative investment strategy, increased returns would, in the long run, make up for increased spending out of the asset base. However, their investment advisor pointed to studies that have shown that, no matter what a nonprofit's investment strategy, it is virtually impossible to spend more than 5 percent of its assets annually and maintain the underlying value of the fund (net of inflation). And with 25 percent of the assets restricted, it would present even more of a challenge not to quickly erode the other 75 percent. Therefore, even a modest spending increase to 8 or 10 percent could significantly reduce the value of the nonprofit's assets.

After this thorough discussion of options and consequences, the board ultimately decided to resist the pressure for immediate increased spending from the nonprofit's assets. However, it directed its investment committee and advisor to evaluate a more aggressive investment strategy that might produce higher returns, which could fund needed program spending over the next five years. Like an ocean liner, most non-profits' investments and strategies cannot and should not "turn on a dime." This board finally concluded that a slow-and-steady approach was the best course for it to follow.

CONFLICTS OF INTEREST

Laws concerning nonprofit conflicts of interest are intended to provide a governance structure for defining, and in a sense, therefore, allowing such conflicts. Within certain constraints, board members are permitted to loan money to, provide services to, sell property to, and participate in joint ventures with charitable organizations on whose boards they serve.

But when it comes to investing the funds of a nonprofit, board members serve themselves and their organizations best by entirely avoiding any conflict, or appearance of conflict, when possible. Consequently, if you own or work for a professional investment company, the best approach is to not involve your company in providing investment management services to a nonprofit on whose board you serve — even if you are not profiting from those services.

The unique problem of the investment management conflict of interest is that it can adversely impact the board's ability to supervise. It is *much* more difficult for a board or investment committee to do that job adequately if one of its members is performing the underlying service. Everyone's natural tendency is to withhold criticism or probing questions from people who are otherwise friends and colleagues. Therefore, the best, simplest, and least burdensome approach with regard to investment management is simply to avoid any potential for conflict of interest. Choose a position: Be a service provider or be a director, but do not try sit on both sides of the table.

Sometimes, however, particularly for small organizations, avoiding the conflict completely is not possible. For some, their board member/investment manager is so committed to the organization that no one can even imagine not having that person fill both roles. And in fairness to those in that situation, most state conflict-of-interest laws *permit* a board member to excuse himself from voting and thereby avoid a direct conflict when providing services. In that case, it is very important that all parties carefully deal with the potential conflict of interest ahead of time by (1) clearly disclosing the potential conflict to the board, (2) obtaining the board's formal consent, and (3) consistently excusing oneself from any voting on investment matters. In addition, the board member/investment manager should not serve on the investment committee if there is one.

Investment professionals who are not providing services should otherwise be welcome to sit on a board and/or investment committee in order to provide their specialized knowledge and unique viewpoints to the other board members. Such professionals should then be guided by the same conflict-of-interest rules that apply to all members of the board. When the occasion does arise for a professional to influence decisions that would benefit his or her company or him or herself personally (such as approving an investment that his or her company is promoting), then complete disclosure and abstention from participation — in writing, discussion, or voting — should be the guiding principal for one and all.

ACTION QUESTIONS

1. Do we have unambiguous gift-acceptance policies? Have we identified unacceptable gifts?

2. Do we have a set of roles and responsibilities for our investment committee? Are they well understood and carried out appropriately?

3. What is our approach to socially responsible investing?

4. Can we justify our spending policy in terms of meeting the needs of today and remaining sustainable in the future?

5. Do we have a solid conflict-of-interest policy to eliminate private agendas?

5.
Choosing Investment Advisors

The task of finding the right investment professionals can seem daunting. There are a great many choices and the "labels" are confusing. Let's try to simplify the process by breaking it down into its component parts:

- the investment tasks to be performed

- the relationship of service providers to investment structures

- the role and importance of a consultant

A little clarity regarding the relationships between service providers, the tasks to be performed, and the amount of money we have to manage, will make it much easier to actually select appropriate advisors. With that understanding, we will conclude this section by considering ways to find the right advisors.

TASKS TO BE DONE

The investment management process can be broken down into five discrete steps:

1. Establish asset allocation.

2. Make investment selections (choose stocks, bonds, or other instruments).

3. Buy and sell investments (securities brokerage).

4. Maintain custody of the assets.

5. Report on performance.

The first step in effectively choosing advisors is to understand that all combinations of service providers and investment techniques should address all five requirements. Today we can achieve that result a number of different ways, thanks, largely, to the proliferation of investment structures and investment technology over the past 30 years (e.g., mutual funds, index funds, exchange traded funds, brokerage account wrap programs, and computerized performance reporting and analysis). Increasingly, complete packages of investment services are available at almost any asset level.

SERVICE PROVIDERS AND INVESTMENT STRUCTURES

The primary service providers for the five core investment functions are securities brokers (referred to generally as "broker/dealers"), banks and trust companies, and registered investment advisors (sometimes called investment managers). For the most part, these groups reflect particular licensing structures under federal and state securities laws. Consequently, when non–traditional providers, such as insurance companies, attorneys, accountants, or financial planners provide any of these services, they are commonly doing so either as registered investment advisors or through brokerage subsidiaries or affiliates.

Within the five functional areas, only securities brokers (broker/dealers) can actually trade stocks and bonds on exchanges, and only banks, trust companies, or broker/dealers typically provide custody. All of the other functions, however, (asset allocation, investment selection, and performance reporting) are typically provided *both* by registered investment advisors *and* by the broker/dealers and banks, acting in that same capacity. The overlapping service is probably the single biggest source of confusion.

The investment industry also commonly packages the five functions together. When investing in a mutual fund, for example, the fund's advisor selects the securities and then directs the trades through one or more brokers. If the fund company also offers an asset allocation service, custodies the shares, and provides a performance report, then the mutual fund effectively provides all five functions. This is a very efficient option for investors with limited funds, as mutual funds typically accept investments as low as $1,000. Nonprofit organizations commonly use mutual funds when total assets under management are less than $1 million.

"Wrap accounts" represent another approach to providing all five investment functions. A wrap account is an arrangement whereby major brokerage houses offer third-party investment management services with their own custody and trading functions for a single, asset-based fee. Annual wrap fees are graduated, with the highest percentage charged on minimum sized accounts (typically $100,000), then decreasing as the assets under management increase. In addition to investment selection and trading costs, most programs provide multiclass asset allocation services and performance reporting as part of the package. Nonprofit organizations commonly use wrap programs when assets under management range from $500,000 to $25 million.

For very large nonprofits, those with $25 to $100 million dollars or more under management, it becomes cost effective to purchase the various services separately. Thus, larger organizations can retain a consultant to provide asset allocation and performance reporting, contract directly with one or more investment advisors for investment selection, direct the advisors to trade through particular brokers, and custody the assets at one of many large banks. This structure is the norm in the billion dollar endowment world.

Passive Structures and Active Advisors

A fourth and final "structure," arising out of the growing universe of "passive" investment options, also serves to illustrate the increasing flexibility in the industry. Some in the investment world advocate dispensing with advisors in favor of passive investments in index and exchange traded funds. Such funds typically track a specific index, such as the S&P500, so the investment advisor makes no effort to select specific stocks. As a result, index funds have an inherent cost advantage with internal costs and fees that are typically less than one-half of 1 percent. By comparison, fees in traditional, actively managed mutual funds average 1.5 percent or more. A 1 percent cost advantage is significant, especially over time.

Index funds even have a cost advantage over larger, separately managed portfolios. Part of the reason investors use separate managers, as described in the wrap programs above, is a cost advantage over traditional mutual funds. A mutual fund's expense ratio does not usually decline as assets increase and does *not* include the mutual fund's commission costs (whereas wrap-fee programs do). Since traditional mutual funds' trading costs can be 40% of the amount of the expense ratio, separately managed accounts frequently have a significant cost advantage over traditional funds; but the index funds are less expensive still. As the amount of assets under management increase, the cost advantages of index funds diminish but rarely disappear completely. Only for extremely large investors (those in excess of $1 billion dollars) does the index fund cost advantage become negligible.

Index fund proponents also argue that active advisors often do not out-perform indices. The record of active advisors versus index funds is, in fact, mixed. For many years, active advisors (particularly in the largest, most liquid markets) were typically out-performed by index funds. In the recent bear market, however, the situation reversed itself and active advisors out-performed the indices more frequently. It also appears that active advisors are more likely to out-perform in less-well-developed or less liquid markets than in large capitalization markets (such as that represented by the S&P500), for example, small caps or emerging markets.

The fourth structure, therefore, is to utilize allocations to low-cost index funds and exchange-traded funds either in conjunction with or instead of active managers. Many of the providers in the industry including independent registered investment advisors, advisors working for traditional broker/dealers, some of the larger fund families, and some discount brokers are capable of offering this structure. It can be a relatively low-cost approach for small nonprofits.

Finally, it is important to recognize that there are significant reasons beyond cost for using active managers. Those reasons include the following:

1. The conviction of many industry professionals that it is possible to create better, risk-adjusted portfolios by utilizing active managers as opposed to investing in indices. Thus, even the largest and most sophisticated nonprofits continue to use active managers for a majority of their assets.

2. Accommodating necessary tax restrictions, such as investments of a charitable-remainder trust run by a nonprofit. (By avoiding ordinary income and short-term gains in favor of long-term gains, the after-tax value of distributions to beneficiaries can be significantly increased.)

3. Facilitating socially or morally-based investment restrictions that would be impossible to honor in either traditional mutual funds, index, or exchange traded funds.

In addition, active managers are sometimes a source of consulting help.

THE IMPORTANCE AND ROLE OF A CONSULTANT

No matter which investment structure or combination of services an organization selects, someone really needs to act as an overall strategist and advisor. The world of very large institutional accounts has long used so-called consultants to fill this role. Consultants may be registered investment advisors, affiliates of securities brokers or, occasionally, bankers. The only difference for smaller nonprofits is that (largely for cost reasons) the "consultant" might be your broker, your accountant, or your registered investment advisor and not just a separately retained, free-standing advisor.

> **TIP 5:**
>
> Bring your investment manager/advisor to your board meeting to educate all board members on investment issues and to alleviate any concerns about delegation. By meeting the advisor personally, board members feel more secure about their delegation.

No matter what licensing, even small nonprofits should have someone who helps apportion the nonprofit's investment funds to one or more investment managers and/or investment structures. Even if, for cost reasons, we want to exclusively invest through index and exchange traded funds, which ones do we choose?

Just as in the exchange traded fund world there are now hundreds of choices, up from none only a very few years ago.

Utilizing an advisor as a consultant provides a degree of independent oversight, accountability, and performance reporting to the board or investment committee. In addition, such a consultant can provide valuable additional services to board members.

Those services can include evaluating potential gifts of equities or bonds; attending board and committee meetings to explain investment actions, options, and strategies; and even meeting with donors and others to explain an organization's investment policies and approach. At the end of the day, it can be wonderful having such help.

SELECTING AN ADVISOR

The optimal combination of investment management service providers depends on the type and size of your manageable funds, and the sophistication of your investment committee and staff. As an organization's funds increase in size, the continuum of service options grows from (typically) single service providers to specialized providers for every component. The best way to start your search for advisors is to contact the chief financial officers or chief executives of comparably sized organizations in your area and ask for a recommendation. Ask if they have a principal advisor or consultant, whether they have separate brokerage and custodial relationships, and how the actual investments are being implemented (e.g., funds, separately managed accounts, or both). Solicit their comments on and evaluations of advisors they chose — and those they did not. You will soon have a list of candidates to interview.

Be certain that you understand exactly how each service provider is compensated. Each potential advisor should be able to explain in a single, cogent sentence how he will be remunerated for the work he does. Most advisors today are compensated on a fee-for-service basis rather than on a transactional (commission) basis, which is an important improvement. If you understand how and when each provider is compensated, you will be a better judge of any compensation bias that might be contained in the advisor's recommendations.

At the end of this process, you should have identified someone to act as the nonprofit's consultant, charged with the task of advising the chief financial officer, investment committee, and the full board on asset allocation, manager or fund selection, and performance reporting. As we have seen, this service is essential for proper supervision. It can also be a wonderful comfort for board members to not face the complex world of investments alone.

ACTION QUESTIONS

1. What structure or combination of services seems most attractive to us, given the size and complexity of our funds?

2. Do we have a clear idea of the cost of our current investment program?

3. Have we gathered the information we need to search for a consultant in a disciplined process?

6.
21st Century Investment Issues

At the beginning of the 21st century, we are seeing the culmination of a number of worldwide trends affecting the investment environment. They raise important issues and opportunities for nonprofit board members trying to manage assets in that environment. This chapter will examine

- the trend to globalization

- alternative investments for nonprofits

- modern portfolio theory vs. reality

GLOBALIZATION

Normally, I am hesitant to talk about trends because doing so is only half a step removed from making predictions. But globalization is one megatrend that was so well established in the last century and has so much impetus coming into this one, that it is an essential context for any discussion of current investment issues.

For centuries, kings and countries erected barriers to the exchange and sale of goods from the outside. Sometimes enacted to raise tax revenue, sometimes to protect local industries, the effect was the same: to inhibit trade. But since the end of World War II, nations and international organizations have worked steadily and systematically to eliminate those barriers.

The assault on trade barriers has stepped up dramatically in recent years:

- NAFTA (the North American Free Trade Agreement) now largely allows the free flow of goods between the United States, Mexico, and Canada.

- The European Union (EU) has virtually eliminated trade barriers among its members' nations, creating the second largest free-trade zone in the world, and it is actively engaged in reducing trade and agricultural barriers with other regions of the world. The EU has also introduced a new currency, the euro, which is vying with the dollar to become the world's reserve currency.

- The General Agreement on Tariffs and Trade (GATT) is the largest and most comprehensive trade agreement in the world and, in combination with the World Trade Organization, has standardized trade and negotiated the removal of countless tariffs.

While tariffs, trade restrictions, and domestic subsidies remain in place in many countries, the clear trend is toward a world in which there is a free flow of goods and services between nations. Why does this trend matter to nonprofits from an investment perspective? Because the world is so interconnected through trade and finance, there is no longer such a thing as a purely domestic investment. Fifty years ago, it was possible to prudently invest nonprofit funds in portfolios of domestic stocks and bonds without giving the rest of the world a thought. The United States had emerged from World War II as the only major nation with its economy intact and the only nation possessing nuclear weapons. The United States was truly the superpower that dominated the world.

But after the turbulent ensuing 50 years, while the United States remains the only military superpower, it now shares economic power with nations around the world. It is dependent on them to buy U.S. products, to sell low-cost goods and services and, increasingly, to loan money. The extent of globalization and the resulting free and secure flow of capital around the world mean that the disincentives to international investing have largely been removed. Investment capital is increasingly seeking the best returns — wherever those might be generated around the world.

That fact means that most investors — including nonprofits — must open their portfolios to international investments. Simply stated, it is another type of diversification that hedges the risks associated with investing only in the United States. Investing directly in foreign equities and bonds is one way of accomplishing this — although some new dangers, such as currency risks, are thereby introduced into a portfolio. Investing in international mutual funds is another, safer method. A third way, and perhaps the easiest, is to ensure that a portfolio of individual stocks and bonds includes some large, multinational U.S. corporations whose global operations ensure that the portfolio has some international exposure.

The key point is that globalization is a continuing, powerful fact of economic life that must be accommodated by those responsible for nonprofit investing.

ALTERNATIVE INVESTMENTS

One of the interesting developments in recent years has been the increasing use by nonprofits of so-called *alternative investments*. These are usually complicated investment structures, often in partnership format, and usually sold as private placements as opposed to publicly registered securities. (A private placement is a legal way to sell securities to a limited group of purchasers without having to comply with the security-law requirements associated with selling shares to the general public. The theory of private-placement exemption from security laws is that the purchasers will be sophisticated parties who are able to protect themselves.)

Perhaps the best known type of alternative investment is the *hedge fund*. This refers to a broad class of investments that share the following characteristics: (1) they are created in partnership format, (2) they are unconstrained by diversification requirements, and (3) they are typically free to pursue strategies like short selling — the technique of borrowing shares and selling them in the expectation that the shares decline in value. If they do, the short seller buys the shares back and makes a profit from the drop in value. Hedge funds frequently use leverage (usually borrowed funds) and are almost always sold as private placements. There are many subsets within the hedge fund world based on particular strategies, such as market-neutral, distressed-securities, convertible-arbitrage, or event-driven.

Why should a nonprofit organization consider making such a complex investment? The answer is *noncorrelation*. The term, in the financial world, refers to investments that do not respond in the same way to outside economic events. One can greatly reduce one's risk of investment by choosing investments that are noncorrelated. For any given economic event, some of the investments should go up in value and others should go down, thus balancing out one's gains and losses.

However, the risks that are the most difficult to eliminate are those that affect entire markets. For example, if the United States enters a recession virtually all markets decline. The losses in both the S&P500 and the NASDAQ were so enormous during the two years from September 2000 to September 2002 that no amount of intermarket diversification or style-based asset allocation was sufficient to protect one's equity portfolio.

By comparison, the CSFB/Tremont Hedge Fund Index (representing returns for a wide range of hedge funds) actually *increased* 3 to 5 percent each year during this same period of time. The ability of hedge funds to earn returns in poor markets is due to their use of techniques such as short selling. Their potential to add protection against macroeconomic trends is a risk-reduction reason for adding such investments to a portfolio.

As a general rule, alternative investments have a low degree of correlation to the broad market of publicly traded securities. In a recent 10-year period, hedge funds had only a 43 percent correlation to the S&P500. In other words, hedge funds moved in concert with the S&P500 less than half of the time.

Certain other asset classes, including cash and bonds, have an even lower correlation to equities, which is why cash and bonds have long been used to reduce risk in portfolios. But while cash and bonds (particularly short- to mid-term bonds) have lower correlations, they also have significantly lower total returns. Thus, risk reduction comes at a fairly high cost. Hedge funds, by comparison, have higher historic returns (though lower than equities) so they offer the prospect of both low correlation and reasonable returns. It is that combination which has led to such interest in alternative investments in recent years.

Hedge funds are not for the faint of heart and they do not come without several important caveats. First, the complexity of hedge funds and other alternatives, such as private equity investments and "managed futures," virtually mandate the use of a specialized investment advisor or consultant.

Second, most alternative investment programs require the investor to have significant assets in order to participate. Because of high minimum participation requirements, alternatives will not be feasible for nonprofits with small investment funds. But those nonprofits with substantial, long-term funds in endowments, pension plans, or other assets with similar time horizons, should consider alternative investments as part of their portfolios. With caution and in appropriate amounts, they have the potential for further reducing portfolio risks.

MODERN PORTFOLIO THEORY VS. REALITY

In March 2000, the U.S. stock markets achieved their all-time highs. The Dow Jones Industrial Average reached 11,723, the S&P500 exceeded 1,527, and the NASDAQ closed above 5,000 for the first and only two days in its history. The NASDAQ's close was particularly spectacular because that index had increased 300 percent in just 18 months.

This run-up — perhaps better described as a frenzy — was greater than any in living memory. The overwhelming sentiment of most investors, big and small, was that the good times would continue indefinitely. Well-known, respected investment advisors were not immune. Many talked of Internet technology as a new paradigm in which traditional concepts such as sales, revenues, and profits no longer mattered. Company shares were recommended based on multiples of projected future sales, and for products that did not yet exist. New expressions were coined such as "burn rate," which was applied to the consumption of IPO-generated cash.

It seems clear in retrospect that the long decade of prosperity and expansion led many people to forget history, to dismiss the inherent cyclical nature of investing, and to believe that the laws that have governed investing for centuries had been suspended in the "new economy."

Fast-forward to early 2003: The market had been declining for more than 36 months. The NASDAQ had fallen more than 65 percent and the S&P500 almost 50 percent from their former highs. (Although both rallied considerably later in 2003, neither has yet approached their former highs.) The declines left many nonprofits shell-shocked as they watched their assets shrink dramatically over those three years.

But did it have to be that way? Was it possible to come through unscathed? Most importantly, what does this experience mean to nonprofit managers for the future? Is the lesson that nonprofits should minimize investment risks at all costs?

When we examine the bear market of 2000–2003, we first observe that those hurt the worst had most aggressively invested in the technology boom of the late 1990s. Anyone who invested heavily in a single tech company stock, for example, could easily have lost 95 percent or more of his or her entire investment. Similarly, there were a number of mutual funds (many of which are no longer in business) that invested in narrow segments of the stock market, such as shares of Internet companies or telecom stocks. Again, participating investors might easily have lost 90 percent or more of their portfolios.

Those investors were hurt so badly because they were highly undiversified and thereby exposed to either single-company or single-sector risk. To the extent that avoiding that level of damage is the standard, portfolio theory as expressed in broad diversification and asset allocation was effective at reducing investment losses.

But, was it possible to come through unscathed? If the definition of unscathed is "not experiencing any adverse consequences from a three-year bear market," then the answer is probably no. To do that, one would have to have been 100 percent invested in bonds or cash near the peak of the market — and such market timing is notoriously difficult to execute.

It would also have been extremely unlikely that anyone would have pursued this strategy since an all-fixed-income portfolio does not have nearly the same potential total return as does a portfolio with some equity allocation. Further, so long as there is either a significant level of inflation, low interest rates, or the possibility of future inflation, it is highly questionable whether an all-bond allocation could be defended for long-term investment funds.

But if the definition of unscathed is "emerge from the bear market without experiencing punishing losses, while at the same time having significant equity investments," then the answer is yes. The chart below illustrates the performance of the S&P500; the NASDAQ; and a balanced growth portfolio for the three years ending September 30, 2002 (covering the period of the peak run-up and the subsequent market decline). The model growth portfolio held 55% equities, 25% fixed income, 5% cash, and 15% in hedge funds. The equities were also broadly diversified by asset class and style. Just a glance at the chart shows the impressive benefit of including bonds, cash, and hedge funds in a "growth" portfolio. While a 3 percent total return over 36 months (the return of the model portfolio in the chart) is not normally something to celebrate, when compared to the dramatic 67 percent loss experienced by the NASDAQ, it seems like a divine gift.

Relative Performance of Diversified Portfolio

September 1999 through September 2002

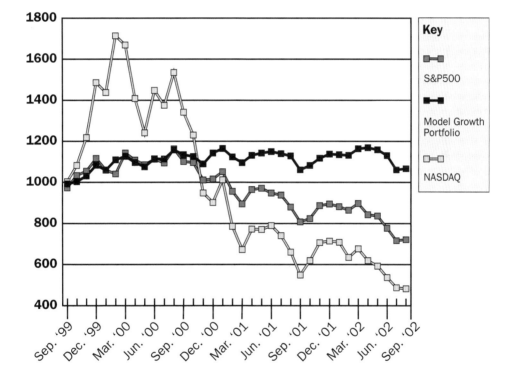

Smaller nonprofits might question the impact of the hedge fund allocation in the Model Growth Portfolio. Was that allocation the source of the "protection" of this portfolio during the market's decline? The answer is that the hedge funds helped — slightly — but that most of the downside protection came from the allocation to bonds and cash. Even more to the point, the downside protection came from not having more than 55% of the portfolio allocated to equities. A portfolio allocated 55% to equities and 45% to fixed income and cash would also have held up well during this period.

The conclusion to which the illustration points is that it was possible to come through one of the worst market declines without crippling losses by employing modern portfolio techniques. But this review of what might have been is not intended to reopen old wounds. In fairness, even a great many well-advised organizations suffered greater losses than they thought possible in the market's downturn. Many of us as advisors, for example, recommended higher equity allocations than 55% for some clients' endowments and other permanent funds. Those clients' portfolios did not perform as well as the model growth portfolio on the chart.

The important point — the point not to miss — is that the principal tools of modern portfolio theory — diversification and asset allocation — when practiced with sufficient breadth, did protect portfolios against excessive losses. Diversification alone does not get the job done. Even asset allocation can be inadequate if, for example, all of the classes being used are components of the S&P500. But the two tools together, with asset classes that include fixed income, cash, international securities, real estate securities, and other noncorrelated asset classes when possible, can reduce portfolio risk. Returning to our very first thoughts — since we must invest — we ought to do so in the safest way possible that still offers a reasonable chance of achieving our goals. That is the point of modern portfolio theory.

TIMELESS CONCEPTS

After looking deeper into the issues of the 21st century (thus far) in investment management, here are a few observations on timeless concepts that all investors — including nonprofit board members — should keep in mind.

LIMITATIONS OF THE HISTORICAL RECORD

Always remember that there is a largely unspoken assumption in the investment world that past behavior and experiences are an accurate guide to the future. Virtually all analytic investment techniques, including asset allocation, are based on historic performance. When judging the reliability of predictions or recommendations that are made to you, it is healthy to keep this limitation in mind. History can be a guide, but it does not often precisely repeat itself.

ABSOLUTE VS. RELATIVE RETURNS

Nonprofits too often invest expecting an absolute return from their investments — because they want or need to earn a particular level to achieve their goals. A more realistic view is always to look first at your returns relative to the market or some subset of the market. As a nonprofit director, hold on to your absolute return goals, but expect only relative goals to be fulfilled.

DIFFICULTY OF MAKING JUDGMENT CALLS

Give yourself room to make bad judgment calls. The unfortunate reality is that even the best investment techniques are not all that precise. Something as fundamental as assessing an organization's tolerance for risk cannot easily be reduced to numbers or formulas. Judgment is involved in determining what level of potential losses could in fact be absorbed and human fallibility is always present in the judgments we make.

ACTION QUESTIONS

1. Do our diversification efforts take adequately into account the benefits and risks of globalization and international investments?

2. Are we in full agreement about restrictions concerning alternative investment options?

3. Do we have realistic performance expectations of our investments?

4. Do we periodically reassess our investment approach and rebalance the portfolio?

Conclusion

The purpose of this material is to help board members with the responsibility for supervising the investments of a nonprofit. As we have seen, investment advisors cannot do their best for an organization without board members' willingness to learn, active supervision, and support. Having processes in place by which to routinely convey to an advisor your goals, objectives, and attitudes toward risk, and by which you routinely receive information on strategies, results, and specific investments is the essential component of a well-managed nonprofit investment portfolio.

The world of investing is shockingly unrestrained, compared to almost any other modern discipline or profession. The securities laws are designed not to curb or constrain investments, but simply to require disclosure to potential investors. Add to that the uncertainty of the world today — the assumptions on which investment decisions are made can be altered with a terrorist bomb or a new tariff — and it may seem like a strange world for a nonprofit organization to enter. But, as we have seen, it is a world that each nonprofit must enter at some level, whether it is choosing where to put a $5,000 checking account or a $5 billion endowment.

As a board member of a nonprofit organization, you are charged with doing a responsible job in regard to investment of the nonprofit's assets. The thread that runs through this book is the belief that the average person — men and women who are not investment professionals — can and should provide guidance and oversight to the investment process of the organizations on whose boards they serve. At the end of the day, there is no substitute for the good judgment that the average board member can bring to the process. There is no substitute for the board member who is willing to ask the obvious questions and apply old-fashioned common sense. If you are willing to ask those questions and apply your sound reasoning powers to the answers, you will serve your organization exceptionally well — and establish a lasting legacy for the future.

Appendix I

SAMPLE INVESTMENT POLICIES

Please see the attached CD-ROM for a downloadable and customizable version of the following sample policies.

SAMPLE INVESTMENT POLICIES — GENERAL

The following is a basic set of investment policies for a charitable organization. It establishes an investment committee and authorizes the retention of an investment consultant to guide and assist the committee in its work. It then addresses all of the standard investment policy issues. Please note, however, that this form is only a sample and may not be appropriate for any specific organization without significant modifications and additions. In that regard, this particular set of policies is intended to be helpful primarily to smaller organizations and those adopting policies for the first time, as opposed to organizations with larger or well-established investment operations. When drafting policies, you would ideally do so in conjunction with your investment consultant and should always have such policies reviewed by your legal counsel before adoption.

Preamble

It is the policy of the Board of Directors (Board) to treat all assets of the Nonprofit Organization (NPO), including Funds which are legally unrestricted, as if held by NPO in a fiduciary capacity for the sake of accomplishing its mission and purposes. The following investment objectives and directions are to be judged and understood in light of that overall sense of stewardship. In that regard, the basic investment standards shall be those of a prudent investor as articulated in applicable state laws.

Investment Assets

For purposes of these policies, investment assets are those assets of NPO which are available for investment in the public securities markets as stocks, bonds, cash, or cash equivalents, either directly or through intermediate structures. Illiquid assets are described in NPO's Gift Acceptance Policies, and are governed by those rules and not by these investment policies.

Supervision and Delegation

The Board of Directors of NPO has adopted these policies and has formed an Investment Committee, described below, to whom it has delegated authority to supervise NPO investments. The Board reserves to itself the exclusive right to amend or revise these policies.

Investment Committee

The Investment Committee ("Committee") is comprised of the chief financial officer, _____, Board members and _____ non–board member(s), who serve at the pleasure of the Board. It shall be the responsibility of the Committee to:

1. Supervise the overall implementation of NPO's investment policies by NPO's executive staff and outside advisors;

2. Monitor and evaluate the investment performance of NPO's Funds;

3. Report regularly on NPO investment matters to the Board of Directors;

4. Grant exceptions as permitted in these policies and recommend changes in approved policy, guidelines, and objectives as needed; and,

5. Execute such other duties as may be delegated by the Board of Directors.

Whenever these policies assign specific tasks to the Committee, the policies assume that the actual work will (or may) be performed by NPO's chief financial officer or other designated staff members, subject only to the Committee's overall supervision.

Investment Consultant, Advisors, and Agents

The Committee is specifically authorized to retain one or more investment advisors (Advisors) as well as any administrators, custodians, or other investment service providers required for the proper management of NPO's Funds. The Committee may utilize an Advisor as an investment consultant (the "Consultant") to advise and assist the Committee in the discharge of its duties and responsibilities. In that regard, a Consultant may help the Committee to:

1. Develop and maintain investment policy, asset allocation strategies, risk-based fund objectives, and appropriate investment management structures;

2. Select, monitor, and evaluate Investment Advisors and/or investment entities;

3. Provide and/or review quarterly performance measurement reports and assist the Committee in interpreting the results;

4. Review portfolios and recommend actions, as needed, to maintain proper asset allocations and investment strategies for the objectives of each fund; and,

5. Execute such other duties as may be mutually agreed.

In discharging this authority, the Committee can act in the place and stead of the Board and may receive reports from, pay compensation to, enter into agreements with, and delegate discretionary investment authority to such Advisors. When delegating discretionary investment authority to one or more Advisors, the Committee will establish and follow appropriate procedures for selecting such Advisors and for conveying to each the scope of their authority, the organization's expectations, and the requirement of full compliance with these Policies.

Objectives

NPO's primary investment objective is to preserve and protect its assets, by earning a total return for each category of assets (a "Fund"), which is appropriate for each

Fund's time horizon, distribution requirements, and risk tolerance. NPO currently maintains [list Funds here, e.g., Operating Reserves, Endowments, Charitable Trust Funds, Annuity Reserves] and may add other Funds in the future. These policies apply to all NPO Funds, although the specific objectives, risk parameters, and asset allocation will vary, as appropriate, from Fund to Fund.

Asset Allocations

Actual asset allocations for each Fund will be established and maintained by NPO on the advice of its Consultant and/or Advisors, within the ranges provided in the following table:

(Sample Only)

Investment Fund	Asset Class		
	Equities	Fixed-Income	Cash and Cash Equivalents
Operating Reserves	0%	0–50%	50–100%
Annuity Reserves	30–60%	35–75%	5–35%
Charitable Trusts	30–60%	35–75%	5–35%
Endowments	50–80%	15–50%	5–20%

When appropriate, specific objectives for each Fund, including specific asset allocation parameters and performance standards, may be reflected in an appendix attached to these policies. Such specific objectives shall nonetheless be within the foregoing ranges which can only be modified by the Committee with the approval of the Board.

Rebalancing Procedures

The Committee will monitor the asset allocation of each Fund based on reports provided by NPO's Consultant and/or Investment Advisors. The Committee may establish any reasonable rebalancing procedure based on either periodic reviews or departures from a range and may use its discretion to determine the timing of rebalancing actions. To achieve rebalancing, NPO may either move money from one asset class to another or may direct future contributions and expenditures from particular classes as is most convenient.

Investment Guidelines

To accomplish its investment objectives, NPO is authorized to utilize any legal investment structure including separately managed portfolios, mutual funds, exchange traded funds, limited partnerships, and other commingled investment entities. This authority is subject to the requirements and restrictions contained in these policies.

When utilizing mutual funds or other commingled entities, the Committee shall see that NPO's staff, Consultant, and/or Investment Advisors have selected the investment entity appropriately based on the strategies and provisions contained in the entity's prospectus. In that event, the terms and conditions of the prospectus are deemed to control the entity's internal asset allocation, asset quality, diversification, and other requirements.

For separately managed portfolios, the following additional requirements shall apply:

Asset Quality

1. Common stocks — The Advisor may invest in any unrestricted, publicly traded common stock that is listed on a major exchange or a national, over-the-counter market, and that is appropriate for the portfolio objectives, asset class, and/or investment style of the Fund that is to hold such shares.

2. Convertible preferred stock and convertible bonds — The Advisor may use convertible preferred stocks and bonds as equity investments. The quality rating of convertible preferred stock and convertible bonds must be BBB or better, as rated by Standard & Poor's; or BAA or better, as rated by Moody's;rM. The common stock into which both may be converted must satisfy the standard of Section 1, above.

3. Fixed-income securities — The quality rating of bonds and notes must be A or better, as rated by Standard & Poor's or Moody's;rM. The portfolio may consist of only traditional principal and interest obligations with maturities of _____ (e.g., seven) years or less. The Advisor may not utilize derivatives without the prior permission of the Committee.

4. Short-term reserves — The quality rating of commercial paper must be A+1, as rated by Standard & Poor's, P+1, as rated by Moody's;rM, or better. The assets of any money market mutual funds must comply with the quality provisions for fixed-income securities or short-term reserves.

5. Other securities — The Advisor may invest in real estate investment securities (REITs), international securities traded in the United States directly or as depositary shares, international securities traded on recognized foreign exchanges, and any other publicly traded investments that the Committee determines to be appropriate.

Asset Diversification

The Advisor will maintain reasonable diversification at all times. The equity securities of any one company should not exceed 5 percent of the portfolio at the time of purchase and the combined debt and equity securities should not exceed 10 percent of the portfolio at any time. The Advisor shall also maintain reasonable sector allocations. In that regard, the maximum allocation to any one economic sector shall be 150% of the sector's weighting, as defined in the published index used for measuring the portfolio's performance (e.g., S&P500, Russell 1000, etc.). These restrictions do not apply to U.S. Government securities.

Proxy Voting

Subject to any specific instructions received from NPO or contained in NPO's mission guidelines (see Mission-Based Investment Criteria on the next page), each Advisor shall vote proxies according to their firm's established procedures and shall provide a copy of such procedures to the Committee upon request.

Custody and Securities Brokerage

The Committee will establish such custodial and brokerage relationships as are necessary for the efficient management of NPO's Funds. Whenever the Committee has not designated a brokerage relationship, then NPO Investment Advisors may execute transactions wherever they can obtain best price and execution.

Cash Flow Requirements

NPO will be responsible for advising the Consultant and each Advisor in a timely manner of NPO's cash distribution requirements from any managed portfolio or Fund. Each Advisor is responsible for providing adequate liquidity to meet such distribution requirements.

Investment Restrictions

NPO's investment assets are to be managed with regard to the following restrictions for either tax, risk, or mission purposes:

Tax-Based Restrictions

NPO is a charitable organization under § 501(c)(3) of the Internal Revenue Code. Consequently, its income is generally exempt from Federal and State income tax with the exception of income that constitutes Unrelated Business Taxable Income (UBTI). Since UBTI can be generated by leveraged investments (resulting in "debt-financed income"), NPO will not utilize margin, short selling, or other leveraged investment strategies unless the Investment Committee grants a specific exception as described below.

Risk-Based Restrictions

NPO will not engage in commodities transactions or option strategies (puts, calls, straddles) nor will it invest in any non–publicly traded securities including but not limited to managed futures funds, hedge funds, private equity funds, or other alternative investments unless approved by the Committee as provided below.

Mission-Based Investment Criteria

NPO desires to invest in companies whose business conduct is consistent with NPO's goals and beliefs. Therefore, NPO's Consultant and/or Investment Advisors will use their best efforts to avoid holding securities of any company known to participate in businesses the Board deems to be socially or morally inconsistent with NPO objectives. The Committee will provide Advisors with a statement of NPO's mission guidelines and restrictions.

Exceptions to the Investment Restrictions

The Board recognizes the evolving nature of the investment world and that, under some circumstances, NPO may wish to utilize newer or more complex investment strategies. Therefore, the Investment Committee is authorized to grant exceptions to the foregoing restrictions. For tax-based restrictions, the Committee is to determine if a particular strategy or investment will generate UBTI, for which it may rely on advice of counsel. When granting exceptions, the Committee must determine that the potential rewards outweigh the incremental risks. All such exceptions shall be made in writing and shall be communicated to the Board as part of the next regular Investment Committee report.

Reporting Requirements

1. Monthly — The Committee will obtain written monthly custodial statements. Such statements should contain all pertinent transaction details for each account that holds all or a portion of any NPO investment Funds. Each monthly statement should include:

   - the name and quantity of each security purchased or sold, with the price and transaction date; and,

   - a description of each security holding as of month-end, including its percentage of the total portfolio, purchase date, quantity, average cost basis, current market value, unrealized gain or loss, and indicated annual income (yield) at market.

   In addition, if not included in the custodial reports, the Consultant and/or the Investment Advisor(s) should provide a report for each Fund or portfolio showing the month-end allocation of assets between equities, fixed-income securities, and cash. The monthly review of custodial statements may be delegated to NPO accounting staff.

2. Quarterly — The Committee should obtain from its Investment Consultant and/or Investment Advisors, a detailed review of NPO's investment performance for the preceding quarter and for longer trailing periods as appropriate. Such reports should be provided as to each Fund and as to NPO investment assets in the aggregate. As to each Fund, the Committee should establish with its Investment Consultant and/or Investment Advisors the specific criteria for monitoring each Fund's performance including the index or blend of indices that are appropriate for the objectives of each Fund and for the investment style or asset class of each portfolio within a Fund. The Committee shall meet with the Consultant to conduct such reviews to the extent it deems necessary.

3. Periodically — The Committee should meet with its Investment Consultant at least annually to review all aspects of NPO's investment assets. Such a review should include (1) strategic asset allocation, (2) manager and investment entity performance, (3) anticipated additions to or withdrawals from Funds, (4) future investment strategies, and (5) any other matters of interest to the Committee.

SAMPLE INVESTMENT OBJECTIVES FOR OPERATING RESERVES

The following material (pages 49–51) provides samples of the greater level of detail that can be applied to specific Fund objectives if helpful. The operating reserve appendix is for organizations with significant reserves relative to their regular cash flow requirements and illustrates one approach to increasing returns on such funds.

Operating Reserve Objective

The primary Operating Reserve Investment Objective is to optimize yield on NPO's short-term assets while maintaining adequate liquidity and without taking excessive principal risk. To achieve these objectives, NPO's Operating Reserves will be allocated into three tiers designed to meet the specific safety, liquidity, and yield criteria. Those categories are: Operating Funds, Liquid Assets, and Fixed Income Assets, each of which is defined below.

Tier 1 — Operating Funds
The purpose of this tier is to assure adequate cash for operations. To achieve this goal, the Committee (acting through its designated agents) will match Tier 1 investment maturities to the organization's cash flow and draw-down requirements. In no event, however, will Tier 1 maturities exceed 180 days.

Tier 2 — Liquid Assets
The purpose of this tier is to provide a liquidity reserve above and beyond the cash for operations maintained in Tier 1. When investing liquid assets, the Advisor will emphasize safety, liquidity, and yield, in that order, with staggered maturities to a maximum of (12/24) months. The weighted average duration of Tier 2 assets shall be less than [2/3] years.

Tier 3 — Fixed Income Assets
This portion of the operating reserve portfolio is designed to maximize return, consistent with safety of principal. Liquidity is a secondary objective. Maturities should be reasonably laddered out to a maximum of (36/48/60) months. The weighted average duration of Tier 3 assets shall be less than [3/4] years. It is acceptable for there to be some principal fluctuation and risk in this tier in an effort to earn a greater total return.

Maintenance of Tiers
The Committee will periodically determine the allocations to each tier based on prior years' cash-flow and reserve levels as well as anticipated future spending. In making these allocations, they may rely on the cash flow projections of the designated financial officer. The initial amounts to be maintained in each tier are as follows:

OPERATING RESERVE TIERS *(Sample Only)*

Tier	Description	Primary Purpose	Amount
3	Fixed Income Assets	Incremental total return with safety	$1,000,000
2	Liquid Assets	Incremental yield with liquidity	$1,000,000
1	Operating Funds	Ready cash for X months of operations (e.g., 6)	All $ in excess Tiers 2 and 3, but never less than $_____

Cash Flow Management

NPO's designated financial officer will be responsible for managing NPO's cash-flow and for communicating anticipated distributions and liquidity requirements in a timely manner to NPO's Consultant and/or Investment Advisors who are managing the Tiers.

Asset Quality

Within the three tiers described previously, investments shall be made exclusively with the following securities, each of which shall conform to the stated quality requirements:

ASSET QUALITY AND DIVERSIFICATION GUIDELINES			
Instrument	Tier Targets	Quality and Diversification Guidelines	Permitted Maturities
U.S. Treasury Securities	Tiers 1, 2, and 3	$500,000 per issue maximum; Treasuries and agencies should comprise at least 50% of portfolio	60 months or less, subject to more restrictive Tier Requirements
U.S. Government Agency Securities	Tiers 1, 2, and 3	$500,000 per issue maximum; Treasuries and agencies should comprise at least 50% of portfolio	60 months or less, subject to more restrictive Tier Requirements
U.S. Corporate Debt	Tiers 1, 2, and 3	Minimum A rating; $500,000 per issuer maximum; 15% limit on bonds rated A	36 months or less, subject to more restrictive Tier Requirements
Commercial Paper	Tiers 1 and 2	Rated P-1/A-1; $500,000 per issuer maximum	270 days or less
Certificates of Deposit	Tiers 1 and 2	Institution rated A or better; $100,000 per issuer maximum; FDIC insured	12 months or less (except for negotiable CD's which are subject to the U.S. Corporate Debt restriction)
Bankers Acceptances	Tiers 1 and 2	Institution rated A or better; $500,000 per issuer maximum	270 days or less
Repurchase Agreements	Tier 1	U.S. Treasury collateral only	Overnight only
Money Market Funds	Tier 1	Unrestricted	Daily demand

Endowment Fund Objective

The primary Endowment Fund objective is to seek a total return adequate to support a trailing 5 percent spending policy and to maintain the purchasing power of the endowment, net of inflation. Distributions will be made from the Fund quarterly and may be taken from principal or income so there is no requirement to generate a particular level of dividends or interest. The time horizon is perpetual and the Board is not concerned with intermediate volatility. The Fund is nonetheless to be balanced with fixed income instruments in order to reduce the risk of substantial drops in principal value, which could cause public relations problems.

Endowment Fund Asset Allocation (*Sample Only*)

Asset Class/Investment Style	Minimum	Target	Maximum
Domestic Large Capitalization Equity	30%	35%	40%
Domestic Small/Medium Capitalization Equity	7%	10%	13%
International Equity	15%	20%	25%
Real Estate Securities	3%	5%	7%
Total Equity	**55%**	**70%**	**85%**
Intermediate-Term Fixed Income	5%	20%	25%
Short-Term Fixed Income	5%	5%	13%
Cash and Cash Equivalents	5%	5%	7%

Endowment Fund Performance Indices (*Sample Only*)

Endowment Fund Balanced Objective	Percentage	Index
	35%	Standard & Poor's 500 Stock Index
	15%	Russell 2000 Stock Index
	20%	Morgan Stanley Capital International Europe, Australasia and Far East (MSCI EAFE) International Stock Index
	20%	Merrill Lynch Intermediate Corporate/Government Bond Index
	5%	Merrill Lynch 1–5 year Corporate/Government Bond Index
	5%	90 day Treasury Bills

Appendix II

SAMPLE SPENDING POLICY

Please see attached CD-ROM for a downloadable and customizable version of the following sample policy.

The Fund shall annually distribute an amount equal to five percent (5%) of the Fund's average value as calculated in this paragraph. The distributions shall be made quarterly in an amount equal to one and one-quarter percent (1.25%) of the calculated Distribution Value. The Distribution Value is the average of the fair market value of the Fund as of the close of each of the preceding 12 calendar quarters. The Fund's market value shall be based upon all assets in the Fund including principal and retained income, adjusted for all gains and losses, whether realized or unrealized, and determined as of the last business day of the quarter. The distributions shall be made promptly following the close of each quarter. To the extent that it may legally do so, the organization shall interpret this policy as satisfying a gift provision which calls for retaining principal and distributing income.

Appendix III

UNIFORM MANAGEMENT OF INSTITUTIONAL FUNDS ACT

Please see the attached CD-ROM for an electronic copy of UMIFA.

An Act to establish guidelines for the management and use of investments held by eleemosynary institutions and funds.

Section

1. Definitions
2. Appropriation of Appreciation
3. Rule of Construction
4. Investment Authority
5. Delegation of Investment Management
6. Standard of Conduct
7. Release of Restrictions on Use or Investment
8. Severability
9. Uniformity of Application and Construction
10. Short Title
11. Repeal

Be it enacted ... ...

§ 1. Definitions

In this Act:

(1) "institution" means an incorporated or unincorporated organization organized and operated exclusively for educational, religious, charitable, or other eleemosynary purposes, or a governmental organization to the extent that it holds funds exclusively for any of these purposes;

(2) "institutional fund" means a fund held by an institution for its exclusive use, benefit, or purposes, but does not include (i) a fund held for an institution by a trustee that is not an institution or (ii) a fund in which a beneficiary that is not an institution has an interest, other than possible rights that could arise upon violation or failure of the purposes of the fund;

(3) "endowment fund" means an institutional fund, or any part thereof, not wholly expendable by the institution on a current basis under the terms of the applicable gift instrument;

(4) "governing board" means the body responsible for the management of an institution or of an institutional fund;

(5) "historic dollar value" means the aggregate fair value in dollars of (i) an endowment fund at the time it became an endowment fund, (ii) each subsequent donation to the fund at the time it is made, and (iii) each accumulation made pursuant to a direction in the applicable gift instrument at the time the accumulation is added to the fund. The determination of historic dollar value made in good faith by the institution is conclusive.

(6) "gift instrument" means a will, deed, grant, conveyance, agreement, memorandum, writing, or other governing document (including the terms of any institutional solicitations from which an institutional fund resulted) under which property is transferred to or held by an institution as an institutional fund.

§ 2. Appropriation of Appreciation

The governing board may appropriate for expenditure for the uses and purposes for which an endowment fund is established so much of the net appreciation, realized and unrealized, in the fair value of the assets of an endowment fund over the historic dollar value of the fund as is prudent under the standard established by Section 6. This Section does not limit the authority of the governing board to expend funds as permitted under other law, the terms of the applicable gift instrument, or the charter of the institution.

§ 3. Rule of Construction

Section 2 does not apply if the applicable gift instrument indicates the donor's intention that net appreciation shall not be expended. A restriction upon the expenditure of net appreciation may not be implied from a designation of a gift as an endowment, or from a direction or authorization in the applicable gift instrument to use only "income," "interest," "dividends," or "rents, issues, or profits," or "to preserve the principle intact," or a direction that contains other words of similar import. This rule of construction applies to gift instruments executed or in effect before or after the effective date of this Act.

§ 4. Investment Authority

In addition to an investment otherwise authorized by law or by the applicable gift instrument, and without restriction to investments a fiduciary may make, the governing board, subject to any specific limitations set forth in the applicable gift instrument or in the applicable law other than law relating to investments by a fiduciary, may:

(1) invest and reinvest an institutional fund in any real or personal property deemed advisable by the governing board, whether or not it produces a current return, including mortgages, stocks, bonds, debentures, and other securities of profit or nonprofit corporations, shares in or obligations of associations, partnerships, or individuals, and obligations of any government or subdivision or instrumentality thereof;

(2) retain property contributed by a donor to an institutional fund for as long as the governing board deems advisable;

(3) include all or any part of an institutional fund in any pooled or common fund maintained by the institution; and

(4) invest all or any part of an institutional fund in any other pooled or common fund available for investment, including shares or interests in regulated investment companies, mutual funds, common trust funds, investment partnerships, real estate investment trusts, or similar organizations in which funds are commingled and investment determinations are made by persons other than the governing board.

§ 5. Delegation of Investment Management

Except as otherwise provided by the applicable gift instrument or by applicable law relating to governmental institutions or funds, the governing board may (1) delegate to its committees, officers, or employees of the institution or the fund, or agents, including investment counsel, the authority to act in place of the board in investment and reinvestment of institutional funds, (2) contract with independent investment advisors, investment counsel or managers, banks, or trust companies, so to act, and (3) authorize the payment of compensation for investment advisory or management services.

§ 6. Standard of Conduct

In the administration of the powers to appropriate appreciation, to make and retain investments, and to delegate investment management of institutional funds, members or a governing board shall exercise ordinary business care and prudence under the facts and circumstances prevailing at the time of the action or decision. In so doing they shall consider long- and short-term needs of the institution in carrying out its educational, religious, charitable, or other eleemosynary purposes, its present and anticipated financial requirements, expected total return on its investments, price level trends, and general economic conditions.

§ 7. Release of Restrictions on Use or Investment

(a) With the written consent of the donor, the governing board may release, in whole or in part, a restriction imposed by the applicable gift instrument on the use or investment of an institutional fund

(b) If written consent of the donor cannot be obtained by reason of his death, disability, unavailability, or impossibility of identification, the governing board may apply in the name of the institution to the [appropriate] court for release of a restriction imposed by the applicable gift instrument on the use or investment of an institutional fund. The [Attorney General] shall be notified of the application and shall be given an opportunity to be heard. If the court finds that the restriction is obsolete, inappropriate, or impracticable, it may by order release the restriction in whole or in part. A release under this subsection may not change an endowment fund to a fund that is not an endowment fund.

(c) A release under this section may not allow a fund to be used for purposes other than the educational, religious, charitable, or eleemosynary purposes of the institution affected.

(d) This section does not limit the application of the doctrine of *cy pres*.

§ 8. Severability

If any provision of this Act or the application thereof to any person or circumstances is held invalid, the invalidity shall not affect other provisions or applications of the Act which can be given effect without the invalid provision or application, and to this end the provisions of this Act are declared severable.

§ 9. Uniformity of Application and Construction

This Act shall be so applied and construed as to effectuate its general purpose to make uniform the law with respect to the subject of this Act among those states that enact it.

§ 10. Short Title

This Act may be cited as the "Uniform Management of Institutional Funds Act."

§ 11. Repeal

The following acts and parts of acts are repealed:

(1)

(2)

(3)

UNIFORM MANAGEMENT OF INSTITUTIONAL FUNDS ACT: TABLE OF ADOPTING JURISDICTIONS

Please see the attached CD-ROM for Web access links to the general statutes for each jurisdiction listed below.

Jurisdiction	Statutory Citation
Alabama	§§ 16-61A-1 to 16-61A-8
Arkansas	A.C.A. §§ 28-69-601 to 28-69-611
California	Cal.Probate Code, §§ 18500 to 8509
Colorado	C.R.S.A. §§ 15-1-1101 to 15-1-1109
Connecticut	C.G.S.A. §§ 45a-526 to 45a-534
Delaware	12 Del.C. §§ 4701 to 4708
District of Columbia	D.C. Code 1981, §§ 32-401 to 32-409
Florida	§§ 1010.10-1 to 1010.10-10 (expires 7/1/2004)
Georgia	O.C.G.A. §§ 44-15-1 to 44-15-9
Hawaii	HRS §§ 517D-1 to 517D-11
Idaho	§§ 33-5001 to 33-5008
Illinois	S.H.A. 760 ILCS 50/1 to 10
Indiana	A.I.C. 30-2-12-1 to 30-2-12-13
Iowa	I.C.A. §§ 540A.1 to 540A.9
Kansas	K.S.A. 58-3601 to 58-3610
Kentucky	KRS 273.510 to 273.590
Louisiana	LSA-R.S. 9:2337.1 to 9:2337.8
Maine	13 MRSA §§ 4100 to 4109
Maryland	Code, Estates, Trusts, §§ 15-401 to 15-409
Massachusetts	M.G.L.A. c. 180A, §§ 1 to 11
Michigan	M.C.L.A. §§ 451.1201 to 451.1210
Minnesota	M.S.A. §§ 309.62 to 309.71
Mississippi	§§ 79-11-601 to 79-11-617
Missouri	V.A.M.S. §§ 402.010 to 402.060
Montana	MCA 72-30-101 to 72-30-207

Nebraska	§§ 58-601 to 58-609
Nevada	§§ 164.500 to 164.630
New Hampshire	RSA 292-B:1 to 292-B:9
New Jersey	N.J.S.A. 15:18-15 to 15:18-24
New Mexico	N.M.S.A. §§ 46-9-1 to 46-9-12
New York	N-PCL §§ 102, 512, 514, 522
North Carolina	G.S. §§ 36B-1 to 36B-10
North Dakota	NDCC 15-67-01 to 15-67-09
Ohio	R.C. §§ 1715.51 to 1715.59
Oklahoma	60 Okl.St.Ann. §§ 300.1 to 300.10
Oregon	ORS 128.310 to 128.355
Rhode Island	Gen. Laws 1956, §§ 18-12-1 to 18-12-9
South Carolina	Code 1976, §§ 34-6-10 to 34-6-80
Tennessee	T.C.A. §§ 35-10-101 to 35-10-109
Texas	V.T.C.A., Prop. Code §§ 163.001 to 163.009
Utah	§§ 13-29-1 to 13-29-8
Vermont	14 V.S.A. §§ 3401 to 3407
Virginia	Code 1950, §§ 55-268.1 to 55-268.10
Washington	RCWA 24.44.010 to 24.44.900
West Virginia	§§ 44-6A-1 to 44-6A-8
Wisconsin	W.S.A. 112.10
Wyoming	W.S. 1977, §§ 17-7-201 to 17-7-205

Appendix IV

UNIFORM PRUDENT INVESTOR ACT

Please see the attached CD-ROM for an electronic version of UPIA.

§ 1. Prudent Investor Rule

(a) Except as otherwise provided in subsection (b), a trustee who invests and manages trusts assets owes a duty to the beneficiaries of the trust to comply with the prudent investor rule set forth in the [Act].

(b) The prudent investor rule, a default rule, may be expanded, restricted, eliminated, or otherwise altered by the provisions of a trust. A trustee is not liable to a beneficiary to the extent that the trustee acted in reasonable reliance on the provisions of the trust.

§ 2. Standard of Care; Portfolio Strategy; Risk and Return Objectives

(a) A trustee shall invest and manage trust assets as a prudent investor would, by considering the purposes, terms, distribution requirements, and other circumstances of the trust. In satisfying this standard, the trustee shall exercise reasonable care, skill, and caution.

(b) A trustee's investment and management decisions respecting individual assets must be evaluated not in isolation but in the context of the trust portfolio as a whole and as a part of an overall investment strategy having risk and return objectives reasonably suited to the trust.

(c) Among circumstances that a trustee shall consider in investing and managing trust assets are such of the following as are relevant to the trust or its beneficiaries:

    (1) general economic conditions;

    (2) the possible effect of inflation or deflation;

    (3) the expected tax consequences of investment decisions or strategies;

    (4) the role that each investment of course of action plays within the overall trust portfolio, which may include financial assets, interests in closely held enterprises, tangible and intangible personal property, and real property;

    (5) the expected total return from income and the appreciation of capital;

    (6) other resources of the beneficiaries;

    (7) need for liquidity, regularity of income, and preservation of appreciation of capital; and

    (8) an asset's special relationship or special value, if any, to the purposes of the trust of to one or more of the beneficiaries.

(d) A trustee shall make a reasonable effort to verify facts relevant to the investment and management of trust assets.

(e) A trustee may invest in any kind of property or type of investment consistent with the standards of this [Act].

(f) A trustee who has special skills or expertise, or is named trustee in reliance upon the trustee's reputation that the trustee has special skill or expertise, has a duty to use those special skills or expertise.

§ 3. Diversification

A trustee shall diversify the investments of the trust unless the trustee reasonably determines that, because of special circumstances, the purposes of the trust are better served without diversifying.

§ 4. Duties at Inception of Trusteeship

Within a reasonable time after accepting a trusteeship or receiving trust assets, a trustee shall review the trust assets and make and implement decisions concerning the retention and disposition of assets, in order to bring the trust portfolio into compliance with the purposes, terms, distribution requirements, and other circumstances of the trust, and with the requirements of this [Act].

§ 5. Loyalty

A trustee shall invest and manage the trust assets solely in the interest of the beneficiaries.

§ 6. Impartiality

If a trust has two or more beneficiaries, the trustee shall act impartially in investing and managing the trust assets, taking into account any differing interests of the beneficiaries.

§ 7. Investment Costs

In investing and managing trusts assets, a trustee my only incur costs that are appropriate and reasonable in relation to the assets, the purposes of the trust, and the skills of the trustee.

§ 8. Reviewing Compliance

Compliance with the prudent investor rule is determined in light of the facts and circumstances existing at the time of a trustee's decision or action and not by hindsight.

§ 9. Delegation of Investment and Management Functions

(a) A trustee may delegate investment and management functions that a prudent trustee of comparable skills could properly delegate under the circumstances. The trustee shall exercise reasonable care, skill, and caution in:

(1) selecting an agent;

(2) establishing the scope and terms of the delegation, consistent with the purposes and terms of the trust; and

(3) periodically reviewing the agent's actions in order to monitor the agent's performance and compliance with the terms of delegation.

(b) In performing a delegated function, an agent owes a duty to the trust to exercise reasonable care to comply with the terms of the delegation.

(c) A trustee who complies with the requirements of subsection (a) is not liable to the beneficiaries or to the trust for the decisions or actions of the agent to whom the function was delegated.

(d) By accepting the delegation of a trust function from the trustee of a trust that is subject to the law of this State, an agent submits to the jurisdiction of the courts of this State.

§ 10. Language Invoking Standard of [Act]

The following terms or comparable language in the provisions of a trust, unless otherwise limited or modified, authorizes any investment or strategy permitted under this [Act]: "investments permissible by law for investment of trust funds," "legal investments," "authorized investments," "using the judgment and care under the circumstances then prevailing that persons of prudence, discretion, and intelligence exercise in the management of their own affairs, not in regard to speculation but in regard to the permanent disposition of their funds, considering the probable income as well as the probable safety of their capital," "prudent man rule," "prudent trustee rule," "prudent person rule," and "prudent investor rule."

§ 11. Application to Existing Trusts

This [Act] applies to trusts existing on and created after its effective date. As applied to trusts existing on its effective date, the [Act] governs only decisions or actions occurring after that date.

§ 12. Uniformity of Application and Construction

This [Act] shall be applied and construed to effectuate its general purpose to make uniform the law with respect to the subject of the [Act] among the States enacting it.

§ 13. Short Title

This [Act] may be cited as the "[Name of Enacting State] Uniform Prudent Investor Act."

§ 14. Severability

If any provision of this [Act] or its application to any person or circumstance is held invalid, the invalidity does not affect other provisions or applications of the [Act], which can be given effect without the invalid provision or application, and to this end the provisions of this [Act] are severable.

§ 15. Effective Date

This [Act] takes effect . . . .
. . . .

§ 16. Repeals

The following acts and parts of acts are repealed:

(1)

(2)

(3)

UNIFORM PRUDENT INVESTOR ACT: TABLE OF ADOPTING JURISDICTIONS

Please see the attached CD-ROM for Web access links to the general statutes for each jurisdiction listed below.

Jurisdiction	Statutory Citation
Alaska	§§ 13.36.200 to 13.36.275
Arizona	§§ 14-7601 to 14-7611
Arkansas	§§ 24-2-610 to 24-2-619
California	Cal. Probate Code, §§ 16045 to 16054
Colorado	§§ 15-1.1-101 to 15-1.1 to 115
Connecticut	§§ 45a-541 to 45a-541l
District of Columbia	DC Code, Div. V, Title 28, Subtitle II, Ch. 47, §§ 28-4701 to 28-4712
Florida	§§ 518.11-518.112
Hawaii	§§ 554C-1 to 554C-12
Idaho	I.C. §§ 68-501 to 68-514
Illinois	760 ILCS 5/5, 5/5.1
Indiana	§§ 30-4-3.5-1 to 30-4-3.5-13
Iowa	§§ 633.4301 to 633.4310
Kansas	K.S.A. §§ 58-24a01 to 58-24a19
Maine	18-AM.R.S.A. §§ 7-302, 7-302, note
Massachusetts	203C, §§ 1 to 11
Michigan	§§ 700.1501 to 700.1512
Minnesota	§§ 501B.151, 501B.152
Missouri	§§ 456.900 to 456.913
Nebraska	§§ 8-2201 to 8-2213
New Jersey	§§ 3B:20-11.1 to 3B:20-11.12
New Mexico	§§ 45-7-601 to 45-7-612
New York	Estates, Powers & Trusts § 11-2.3
North Carolina	§§ 36A-161 to 36A-173
North Dakota	(PDF) - §§ 59-02-08.1 to 59-02-08.11
Ohio	§§ 1339.52 to 1339.61

Oklahoma	60 §§ 175.60 to 175.72
Oregon	§§ 128.192 to 128.218
Pennsylvania	20 Pa. C.S.A. §§ 7201 to 7214
Rhode Island	Gen. Laws 1956, §§ 18-15-1 to 18-15-13
Texas	§§ 117.001 to 117.012
Utah	§ 75-7-302
Vermont	9 V.S.A. §§ 4651 to 117.012
Virginia	§§ 26-45.3 to 26-45.14
Washington	§§ 11.100.010 to 11.100.140
West Virginia	§§ 44-6C-1 to 44-6C-15

Appendix V

SELF-GUIDED INVESTMENT AUDIT

This self-assessment form is designed to allow input from multiple staff and committee members. Its questions address all of the issues that an investment consultant would normally consider in preparing an investment strategy. Completing the form will give your organization a very good handle on what you have to manage, your attitudes toward risk, and other factors. Please see the attached CD-ROM for a downloadable and customizable version of the following forms.

Part I: General Information

(This portion is to be completed by the chief executive.)

1. **Institution:** _____

2. **Senior Staff:** **Name**   **Phone**

   Chief Executive   _____   _____
   Senior Development
   Officer   _____   _____
   Chief Financial
   Officer   _____   _____
   Board Chair   _____   _____
   Investment Committee
   Chair   _____   _____

3. **Type of Institution:** School or College   Retirement Home
   Hospital   Church
   Pension Plan   Other Religious Organization
   Public Foundation   Social Service Agency
   Private Foundation   Other Public Charity

4. **Business Structure:** Unincorporated Nonprofit Association
   Nonprofit Corporation (Type) _____
   Limited Liability Company (Type)_____
   Other: _____

5. **Mission Statement:** *(Attach copy or brief narrative description.)*

6. **Approximate Annual Budget:** $_____
   (For reference purposes, please attach a copy of your most recent financial statements.)

7. **Origins:** Founded By: _____   Date:_____
   Founded in (City, State, Country):
   _____

8. **Incorporation:** State:_____   Date:_____

9. Address of Corporate Headquarters: _____

_____

_____

10. Geographic Service Area: *(Describe and list states in which you have at least one full-time employee and a physical location.)*

_____

_____

_____

Part II: Development (Fundraising) Information
(This portion is to be completed by the Senior Development Officer.)

1. Current Staffing of Development Program

Development Staff	Number	
Full-Time Professionals		
Full-Time Support Staff		
Other Staff (Names) who spend some time in Development	Regular position	% of Time Spent in Development

2. What percentage of your organization's total income comes from donations (gifts as opposed to fees for services, sales of products, etc.)?

_____

3. When did you start a full-time fundraising program?

_____

4. When did you start soliciting and/or accepting planned gifts?

_____

5. Please indicate the composition of gift income by category over the last three years.

	Average annual % in last 3 years	Highest annual % in last 3 years	Lowest annual % in last 3 years
Individual Contributions			
Corp. or Foundation Grants			
Bequests			
Lifetime Planned Gifts			
Special Events			
Gifts in Kind; Sponsorships			
Other:			

6. Of the categories listed in the above table, which do you believe are most likely to increase or decrease as a percentage of total annual gift income over the next three years?

Most likely to increase   _____   _____   _____

Most likely to decrease   _____   _____   _____

7. Please rank each of the following areas to indicate your fundraising priorities in terms of the allocation of development staff time for the coming year.

Fundraising Categories	Rank (1st–5th)	Allocable % of Staff Time
Current Annual Giving		
Planned (Deferred) Giving		
Capital Campaign		
Events; Sponsorships		
Corp/Foundation Grants		

8. What are the types, ages, and minimum dollar amounts of the deferred gifts and trusts that your organization accepts?

	Accepted (Y/N)	Minimum Age	Minimum $ Amount
Gift Annuities			
Charitable Remainder Trusts			
Charitable Lead Trusts			
Pooled Income Fund			
Donor-Advised Fund			
Life Interest Agreements in Real Property			
Other:			

9. Please briefly describe the additional staff support, funding, administrative support, or other assistance, if any, that you believe would permit you to more effectively raise funds for your organization over the next three years.

_____

_____

_____

_____

_____

_____

10. Which of the following outside service providers do you currently use in development?

	Organization	Key Contact	First Service (Date)	Address (City, State)	Phone
Fundraising Consultants					
Collateral Material Services					
Securities Broker/Consultant					
Bank or Trust Company					
Investment Advisor					
CPA					
Attorney					
Insurance Agent or CFP					
Other:					

Part III: Investment Accounting, Gift Administration, and Reporting
(This portion is to be completed by the Chief Financial Officer.)

1. What planned gifts, endowments, or other funds does your organization currently have?

Type	No. of Gifts	Total Dollar	Median Size	Oldest Donor	Youngest Donor	Largest Gift – $	Smallest Gift – $
Gift Annuities							
Pooled Income Funds							
Remainder Trusts							
Revocable Trusts							
Operating Reserves							
Endowments							
Retirement Plans							
Capital Campaign Funds							
Other:							

2. How much do you spend administering planned gifts, endowments, or other reserves in each of the following categories: Accounting, Tax Returns, and Investment Management?

	$ Cost	Inside or Out	Service Provider or System Used
Gift Annuities			
Pooled Income Funds			
Remainder Trusts			
Revocable Trusts			
Operating Reserves			
Endowments			
Retirement Plans			
Capital Campaign Funds			
Other:			

3. How do you allocate administrative expenses for each of the following investment instruments (express on a percentage basis)?

	Operating Budget	Charged to Trust or Fund	Comments
Gift Annuities			
Pooled Income Funds			
Remainder Trusts			
Revocable Trusts			
Operating Reserves			
Endowments			
Retirement Plans			
Capital Campaign Funds			
Other:			

4. For each of the following instruments, how frequently do you make income distributions and send reports? Who serves as trustee on the trusts and what information do you provide when reporting?

Key: Frequency: Q = Quarterly, M = Monthly, A = Annual; Reports: 1099, K-1; IP (Investment Performance)

	Trustee	Distributions Frequency	Reports — Frequency and Content
Gift Annuities			
Pooled Income Funds			
Remainder Trusts			
Revocable Trusts			
Operating Reserves			
Endowments			
Retirement Plans			
Capital Campaign Funds			
Other:			

5. Do you have established investment policies for your managed funds? (Y/N).
   Who sets the policies? _____ Are the policies disclosed to your
   donors? (Y/N)

6. Which outside service providers do you currently use in administering your
   planned gift and investment management assets?

	Organization	Key Contact	First Service (Date)	Address (City, State)	Phone
A) Securities Broker/ Consultant					
B) Bank or Trust Company					
C) Investment Advisor					
D) CPA					
E) Attorney					
F) Insurance Agent or CFP					
G) Other:					
H) Other:					

7. Who in your organization is responsible for supervising each of the following areas?

	Name	Phone
Trust Administration	_____	_____
Investment Management	_____	_____
Donor Reporting	_____	_____
Financial Accounting	_____	_____
Regulatory Compliance	_____	_____
Tax Compliance	_____	_____

8. Please indicate which of the service providers (listed in question 6), if any, assist you in the following areas. Write the letter for each provider (See #6) in the space provided.

- Communicating investment options to prospective donors? _____

- Establishing investment objectives and policies? _____

- Constructing planned giving presentations for major donors? _____

- Matching return expectations to spending needs and obligations? _____

- Reporting investment results to donors and management? _____

- Providing information for trustee decisions on risk/return relationships, asset allocation, and other similar issues? _____

- Analyzing investment performance for the benefit of donors and management? _____

- Segregating charitable remainder trust funds for independent management based on category of trust (e.g., income only, income only with make-up, 5%, 8%, etc.)? _____

9. Do you accept gifts of illiquid assets, such as real estate and collectibles?_____

10. Who helps with the management and/or liquidation of such assets?

_____

11. What are the most pressing problems that you face in the areas of trust administration, investment management, or planned gift administration?

_____

_____

Part IV: Investment Philosophy and Objectives

(To be answered by the investment committee of the board or by the full board if there is no committee. For those organizations that maintain multiple funds, these questions should be answered with regard to the endowment or other perpetual or long-term funds.)

Goals and Objectives

1. How would you categorize your overall investment objectives? Choose one.

   _____ Growth — maximum growth of capital with little or no income consideration

   _____ Growth with Income — primarily capital growth with some focus on income

   _____ Balanced — equal emphasis on capital growth and income

   _____ Income Oriented — primary emphasis on income

   _____ Capital Preservation — preserve original value regardless of income or growth

2. What average annual "absolute" rate of return, if any, (as opposed to a return "relative" to a market index) do you consider appropriate for long-term investments?

   _____ % per year   _____ % per year above inflation (CPI)

   _____ Prefer a relative standard

3. Relative to popular stock market indices (such as the S&P500), rank your preferences for portfolio performance; 1 is your strongest preference and 5 is what you least prefer.

   _____ Outperform the market in UP market years.

   _____ Decline less than the market in DOWN market years.

   _____ Outperform the market on average over an extended period, without regard to individual years.

   _____ Match market performance over an extended period.

   _____ Ignore relative performance and focus solely on the absolute return goal(s) identified in question 2, above.

4. Please rank your preference for the following investment performance reporting options from 1 to 5, with 1 being your strongest preference.

   _____ Measuring current return or yield relative to required distributions

   _____ Comparing account returns to an "absolute" percent return target

   _____ "Relative" comparison (comparing the account returns to various market indices)

   _____ Comparing to a "real" return (i.e., exceeds the inflation factor by X%)

   _____ Using "absolute" and "relative" total return measures without regard to yield

5. Please describe any specific return requirements or performance reporting concerns that have not been addressed by the preceding questions.

_____

_____

_____

_____

Risk Questions

6. Please rank the following risks in the order of greatest concern (1 being the highest concern, then 2, etc.).

   _____ The failure to generate enough current income to cover required distributions

   _____ The possibility of not achieving an intended rate of return

   _____ Decreasing purchasing power due to inflation

   _____ Wide swings in the value of our investments over three to five years

   _____ A large drop in the value of any one or more investments, wholly apart from overall portfolio performance

   _____ Other: (Please specify.) _____

7. What is the maximum *percentage* loss you could tolerate in your most aggressively invested portfolio over the following time frames?

   _____ % per quarter _____ % in any two-year period

   _____ % per year   _____ Other: (Please describe) _____

8. What is the maximum *dollar* loss you could tolerate in your most aggressively invested portfolio over the following time frames?

   _____ $ per quarter _____ $ in any two-year period

   _____ $ per year   _____ Other: (Please describe) _____

9. Compared to a broad stock market index such as the S&P500, how much fluctuation can you tolerate in the equity portion of your portfolio any given year?

   _____ Much more fluctuation than the market

   _____ Slightly more fluctuation than the market

   _____ Approximately the same fluctuation as the market

   _____ Slightly less fluctuation than the market

   _____ Much less fluctuation that the market

10. Please describe any risk concerns that the preceding questions have not addressed.

_____

_____

_____

Investment Advisor Questions

11. Which statement best reflects your opinion as to how managers should implement your investment goals?

_____ We should establish overall objectives for the plan and allow the manager complete discretion regarding implementation;

_____ We should establish asset allocation parameters with the investment manager and then allow the manager discretion in selecting investments within those parameters; or,

_____ We should establish asset allocation parameters with the investment manager and then actively participate in and/or supervise the day-to-day selection of investments.

12. How do you feel about giving investment discretion to a third-party investment management firm? Choose one.

_____ Very comfortable   _____ Somewhat uncomfortable

_____ Somewhat comfortable   _____ Very uncomfortable

13. Select the statement that best describes how you currently make investment decisions.

_____ We collect and analyze the facts and make decisions on our own.

_____ Others advise us and we make decisions based on their advice.

_____ Our advisors make the decisions.

14. Please briefly list or describe those aspects of your current investment management process that are working well and those that you believe have problems or could be improved. (Examples include performance, performance reporting, asset allocation, etc.)

Working Well:

_____

_____

Concerns — May Need Improvement: (Write — Over)_____

_____

_____

_____

_____

15. Which of the following outside service providers presently provide your
organization with investment management assistance?

	Organization	Key Contact	First Service (Date)	Address (City, State)	Phone
Securities Broker/Consultant					
Bank or Trust Company					
Investment Advisor					
CPA					
Attorney					
Insurance Agent or CFP					
Other:					
Other:					
Other:					

Part V: Fund Information

(To be completed by the Chief Financial Officer)

Please answer a set of questions for each fund identified in Part II of this questionnaire.

Name of Fund: _____ Type of Fund:_____

1. General Portfolio Objective: (Select one.)

    _____ Capital Preservation — the preservation of capital with returns exceeding risk-free investments. Accordingly, the risk level should be low with minimal price volatility.

    _____ Income — modest growth of capital with the generation of income as the primary objective.

    _____ Growth and Income — primarily oriented toward growth of principal with a minor emphasis on portfolio income. Investments could include equities, debt instruments, and cash or cash equivalents for diversification and risk management.

    _____ Growth — growth of capital. The portfolio will exhibit increased volatility while expecting to outperform equity indices over a market cycle.

    _____ Aggressive Growth — aggressive growth of capital is the primary objective. The portfolio may accept higher volatility associated with aggressive growth while expecting to outperform equity indices over a market cycle.

2. Investment time horizon most appropriate for this account: (Select one.)

    _____ 10 years or more

    _____ Five to 10 years

    _____ Three to five years

    _____ Less than three years

3. Target rates of return: 1 year: ___.___% 3 years: ___.___% 5 years: ___.___%

4. What is the current relative risk tolerance for this fund?

    _____ More fluctuation than the market

    _____ Approximately the same fluctuation as the market

    _____ Less fluctuation than the market

    _____ Relative performance measures are inappropriate for this fund

5. What is the maximum loss you could tolerate in this fund over the following time frames?

    _____ % per quarter

    _____ % per year

    _____ % in any two-year period

6. Is the fund taxable? _____ yes _____ no

7. If the fund is taxable, what is the:

   Income tax rate: ____.____% Capital gains tax rate: ____.____%

8. Other information

   Minimum required annual yield (Div and Interest): $_____

   Anticipated annual contributions: $_____

   Anticipated annual withdrawals: $_____

9. Please list the existing assets and attach a current portfolio statement, if available.

Asset Class	Percent Allocated	Dollar Amount
Cash/Cash Equivalents (includes mutual funds)		
Equities (includes mutual funds)		
Bonds (includes mutual funds)		
Real Estate (includes mutual funds, REITs, etc.)		
Private Placements (includes personal business)		
Other Investments (includes mutual funds)		

10. Indicate the current asset allocation percentages and the permitted range if such targets exist. If a category is prohibited, indicate with a "0" maximum percentage. If a category is required, indicate by stating the same percentage for minimum and maximum.

Asset Class	Current	Minimum	Maximum
Cash/Cash Equivalents			
U.S. Stocks			
Foreign Equities			
U.S. Investment Grade Bonds			
Junk Bonds			
Foreign Bonds			
Real Estate (includes mutual funds, REITs, etc.)			
Private Placements (includes personal business)			
Other Investments (includes mutual funds)			

11. Please describe on an attached page the purpose of this fund, any special income or other requirements, any restrictions on investments, and any special reporting requirements.

Appendix VI

GLOSSARY

alternative investments: these are usually complicated investment structures, not ordinary shares or bonds, often in partnership format, and usually sold as private placements as opposed to publicly registered securities.

asset allocation: the process of allocating investment funds to different asset classes. This is usually done as part of the process of creating a portfolio with certain expected risk and return characteristics.

asset class: any of a number of categories of assets. The broadest categories for investment purposes include cash, equities (stocks), bonds, real estate, and commodities.

bond: a loan in which the borrower commits to pay interest either at regular intervals or at maturity, in addition to repaying the principal amount at a certain date.

capital gain: the excess by which proceeds from the sale of a capital asset exceed the cost basis.

certificate of deposit (CD): a receipt for a deposit of funds in a financial institution that permits the holder to receive interest plus the deposit at maturity.

commercial paper: a short-term unsecured promissory note issued by a finance company or a relatively large industrial firm. The notes ($25,000 minimum) are generally sold at a discount from face value with maturities ranging from 30 to 270 days.

commodity: a generic, largely unprocessed good that can be processed and resold. Commodities traded in the financial markets for immediate or future delivery include grains, metals, and minerals.

common stock: a class of capital stock that has no preference to dividends or any distribution of assets. Common stock normally conveys voting rights and is often termed capital stock if it is the only class of stock that a firm has outstanding. *Common stockholders* are the residual owners of a corporation in that they have a claim to what remains after every other party has been paid. The value of their interest depends on the success of the firm.

convertible security: a security that, at the option of the holder, may be exchanged for another asset, generally a fixed number of shares of common stock. Convertible issues frequently are fixed-income securities such as debentures and preferred stock. Their prices are influenced by both changes in interest rates and the values of the asset into which they may be exchanged.

corporate bond: a bond issued by a corporation, as opposed to a bond issued by the U.S. Treasury or a municipality.

custody: the service of holding financial assets for others. The service typically includes collecting dividends and interest, delivering securities and receiving cash on sales, transferring cash and receiving securities on purchases, and issuing monthly reports — in addition to the safe keeping of the assets.

debt instruments: securities representing borrowed funds that must be repaid. Examples of debt securities include bonds, certificates of deposit, commercial paper, and debentures.

derivative instrument: a financial instrument whose value is based on, and determined by, another security or benchmark such as a stock, bond, futures contract, or commodity. One common example is the separation of the interest payment of a mortgage-backed bond from its principal obligation.

diversification: the process of reducing the risk associated with any one investment by acquiring a group of unrelated investment assets. Effective diversification requires assets on which returns, over time, are not directly related to any other asset in the total investment portfolio. A diversified securities portfolio generally includes 18 to 20 issues of firms that are not similarly affected by the same outside economic events.

dividend: a share of a company's net profits distributed by the company to a class of its stockholders. The dividend is paid in a fixed amount for each share of stock held.

Dow Jones Industrial Average: an index maintained and reviewed by editors of *The Wall Street Journal*, the DJIA is not limited to traditionally defined industrial stocks but serves as a measure of the entire U.S. market. Its averages are unique in that they are price weighted rather than market capitalization weighted. Their component weightings are therefore affected only by changes in the stocks' prices, in contrast with other indexes' weightings that are affected by both price changes and changes in the number of shares outstanding. For the sake of continuity, composition changes are rare, and generally occur only after corporate acquisitions or other dramatic shifts in a component's core business.

endowment: funds established for long-term institutional support from which the organization may typically spend only a limited amount in order to ensure the fund's perpetual existence.

equity: stock — both common and preferred.

exchange traded fund: a type of index mutual fund that issues shares, which trade on an exchange. Exchange traded funds (also called ETF's) have the advantages of index funds plus the daily liquidity of a publicly traded stock, but there are commission charges on purchases and sales. One example is *ishares* issued by the Barclay's Global Investors.

fiduciary: a person or an organization that is entrusted with the property of another party, in whose best interests the fiduciary is expected to act when holding, investing, or otherwise utilizing that party's property. A board member is a fiduciary relative to the business and assets of the corporation.

fixed-income security: a security, such as a bond or preferred stock, that pays a constant income each period. Price changes in a fixed-income security are caused primarily by changes in long-term interest rates.

hedge fund: refers to a broad class of investments that share the following characteristics: (1) they are created in partnership format, (2) they are unconstrained by diversification requirements, and (3) they are typically free to pursue strategies like short selling (the technique of borrowing shares and selling them in the expectation that the shares decline in value). Hedge funds frequently use leverage (usually borrowed funds) and are almost always sold as private placements.

index fund: a mutual fund that intentionally mirrors the holdings of a particular securities index such as the S&P500. Such funds do not attempt to earn incremental returns by selecting securities. Consequently, they are less expensive to maintain and usually have lower turn over than traditional mutual funds.

inflation: a general increase in the price level of goods and services, which reduces the purchasing power of the affected currency.

intermediate-term funds: funds expected to be available in one to five years. They may be invested in fixed-income instruments, such as corporate or government bonds, in maturities that are appropriate for the length of time the funds are available.

investment grade: a designation applied to a bond or other fixed-income investment indicating its suitability for purchase by institutions. Investment-grade designations are made by various rating agencies such as Moody's and Standard & Poor's (S&P), based on the credit worthiness and financial strength of the company issuing the debt. S&P investment grade ratings are AAA, AA, A, and BBB.

junk bond: a high-risk, high-yield debt security that, if rated at all, is graded less than BBB. These securities are most appropriate for risk-oriented investors.

leverage: use of fixed costs (typically borrowed funds) in an attempt to increase the rate of return from an investment by allowing the purchase of larger positions. While leverage can operate to increase rates of return, it also increases the amount of risk inherent in an investment.

liquidity: a position in cash or in assets easily convertible to cash.

long-term funds: funds that always include permanent endowments and may also include retirement assets, gift-annuity reserves, or other funds with a long-term purpose and time horizon.

margin account: a brokerage account that permits an investor to purchase securities on credit and to borrow on securities already in the account. Interest is charged on any borrowed funds, but only for the period of time that the loan is outstanding.

market value: the price at which a security currently can be sold.

money market fund: an open-ended mutual fund that invests in short-term, highly liquid instruments such as treasury bills, commercial paper, banker's acceptances, and negotiable certificates of deposit.

Moody's: a trademark for one of the companies that issues ratings denoting the relative investment quality of corporate and municipal bonds.

mutual fund: open-end funds that are not listed for trading on a stock exchange and are issued by companies that use their capital to invest in other companies. Mutual funds sell their own new shares to investors and buy back their old shares upon redemption. Capitalization is not fixed and normally shares are issued as people want them.

NASDAQ: NASDAQ (National Association of Securities Dealers Automated Quotation System) is a computerized data system run by the National Association of Securities Dealers to provide brokers with price quotations for securities traded over the counter. NASDAQ today is where many leading companies are traded, including Microsoft, MCI, and Northwest Airlines.

noncorrelation: the potential for managed futures funds to perform when traditional markets, such as stocks and bonds, may experience difficulty, thus reducing risk of investment. The degree of noncorrelation of any given managed futures fund will vary — some of the investments should go up in value and others should go down, balancing out one's gains and losses.

operating reserves: any funds being held for general spending within the next 12 months.

opportunity cost: the cost of something in terms of an opportunity forgone, or the value of the next-highest-valued alternative use of that resource.

portfolio theory: the theory of selecting an optimal combination of assets such that the investor secures the highest possible return for a given level of risk or the least possible risk for a given level of return. Using portfolio theory, an investor assembles a group of assets on the basis of how the individual assets interact with one another. Thus, a security would be purchased not on the basis of how that security is expected to perform in isolation but rather on the basis of how that security can be expected to influence the risk and return of the investor's entire portfolio.

preferred stock: a security that shows ownership in a corporation and gives the holder a claim prior to the claim of common stockholders on earnings, and also generally on assets, in the event of liquidation. Most preferred stock issues pay a fixed dividend set at the time of issuance.

principal: capital funds, such as the amount contributed to a trust; the repayment obligation (as opposed to the interest obligation) on a bond; or the amount initially invested in securities by an investor.

private placement: a legal way to sell securities to a limited group of purchasers without having to comply with the security-law requirements associated with selling shares to the general public.

return on investment: a measure of the total return an investor is able to earn (income plus capital appreciation) expressed as a percentage of the amount of his or her investment. Return on investment is calculated by dividing total assets into net profits and may be calculated on either a before-tax or after-tax basis.

risk: within the investment community, "risk" usually means the variability of returns from an investment. The greater the variability (i.e., of dividend fluctuation or of security price), the greater the risk. Since investors are generally averse to risk, investments with greater inherent risk must promise higher expected returns. In more common parlance, risk is the chance of a result that is less than you had expected.

risk-free asset: an asset that has, theoretically, no risk or volatility. Such assets might include treasury bills, money market instruments, and certificates of deposit (under $100,000).

risk-free rate of return: the risk-free rate of return is either a rate at which you could lend money to a risk-free asset such as a treasury bill, or a rate at which you can actually borrow money. The most common measure of so-called risk-free return is the 30-day U.S. Treasury bill.

sector: a group of securities that share certain common characteristics based, generally, on the type of products or services they provide. One common division allocates companies into the following sectors: Basic Materials, Consumer Cyclical, Consumer Non-Cyclical, Energy, Financial Services, Industrial, Technology, and Utilities.

short selling: selling a security that must be borrowed to make delivery. Short selling normally entails the sale of securities that are not owned by the seller in anticipation of profiting from a decline in the price of the securities.

short-term funds: those that might be spent within 12 months and generally should be kept in cash or cash equivalents, such as money market funds.

specific risk: the risk that any one stock can significantly diminish the portfolio's value.

speculation: the taking of above-average risks to achieve above-average returns, generally during a relatively short period of time.

Standard & Poor's Corporation: an investment advisory service that publishes financial data. A subsidiary of McGraw-Hill, the company also rates debt securities and distributes a series of widely followed stock indices.

Standard & Poor's 500 Stock Index (S&P500): an inclusive index made up of 500 stock prices including 400 industrials, 40 utilities, 20 transportation, and 40 financial issues. The Index is constructed using market weights (stock price times shares outstanding) to provide a broad indicator of stock price movements.

time horizon: the time interval over which an investment program is to be completed. An investor's time horizon is very important in determining the types of investments that should be selected.

total return: dividend or interest income plus any capital gain less capital losses and expenses. Total return is generally considered a better measure of an investment's return than dividends or interest alone.

United States government securities: all bonds issued by the U.S. Treasury or other agencies of the U.S. government.

United States Treasury bills: interest-bearing government notes with a term of one year or less and a minimum investment of $10,000.

unrealized gain: the increased market value of an asset that is still being held, compared with the asset's cost of acquisition.

unrealized loss: the reduction in value of an asset that is being held compared with the original cost.

yield: the percentage return on an investment from dividends or interest.

Suggested Resources

Berger, Steven. *Understanding Nonprofit Financial Statements*. Washington, DC: BoardSource, 2003. The newly revised and expanded edition of this best-selling title brings an understanding to key accounting terms and concepts, important benchmarking ratios, and sample nonprofit financial statements. Steven Berger's no-nonsense explanations are helpful for board members, treasurers, finance committee members, and staff who prepare financial information for the board.

Bernstein, Richard. *Navigate the Noise*. New York: John Wiley & Sons, 2001. Written by a top wall street analyst, this resource provides an interesting analysis of the problem with too much information in the modern investment world.

Bonner, William. *Financial Reckoning Day*. New York: John Wiley & Sons, 2003. It is helpful to listen to contrarians and, especially, those who have legitimate concerns that everything is not coming up roses. Bill Bonner is the President of Agoura Publishing and the creator of *The Daily Reckoning*, a widely read contrarian's Internet newsletter.

Cary, William L., and Craig B. Bright. *The Law and Lore of Endowment Funds*. New York: The Ford Foundation, 1969.

Cary, William L., and Craig B. Bright. *The Developing Law of Endowment Funds: The Law and the Lore Revisited*. New York: The Ford Foundation, 1974. These two resources are the seminal studies whose conclusions and recommendations led to the adoption of the Prudent Investor Rule. While technically dated, the thoughts and observations are still interesting and valuable.

Cohen, Jerome, Arthur Zeikel, and Edward D. Zinbarg. *Investment Analysis and Portfolio Management*. Burr Ridge, IL: Irwin, 1987. This resource is one of the standard textbooks on modern portfolio theory. It is a good single volume for those who would like to dig deeper into investment management.

Downes, John, and Jordan Elliot Goodman. *Barron's Finance & Investment Handbook* (6th ed.). Hauppage, NY: Barron's Educational Series, Inc., 2003. This book, useful for both the novice and the more advanced investor, provides a thorough overview of almost every type of investment (including bonds, annuities, life insurance, etc.) and a comprehensive glossary of investment terms. It is handy when it comes to looking up unfamiliar terms and also contains an extensive listing (with contact information) of brokerages, banks, state and federal regulators, major publications, and Web sites.

Ellis, Charles. *Winning the Loser's Game* (4th ed.). New York: McGraw-Hill, 2002. This resource is an excellent little book by a well-known, well-respected investment consultant on the importance of fundamental policy decisions. For those wishing deeper insights from a policy and supervisory perspective, this is a must read.

Foundation for Fiduciary Studies. *Prudent Investment Practices*. New York: American Institute of Certified Public Accountants, 2003. This tool contains many useful references to prudent investment practices for fiduciaries. It provides current insight into the accounting world's view of prudent fiduciary investment practices.

Fry, Robert P. Jr. *Nonprofit Investment Policies: Practical Steps for Growing Charitable, Funds*. New York: John Wiley & Sons, 1998. This book is essentially the "consultants' version" of *Minding the Money*. It addresses the same subjects, focusing specifically on the development of investment policies for nonprofit organizations, but in considerably greater detail. Its purpose is to help those board members, executives, and consultants who are involved in supervising investment policies to approach that task with a greater understanding of the underlying rules and concepts. See also, "Finance & Investments," at www.wiley.com for an interesting selection of books on investing.

Ibbotson, Roger G., and Rex A. Sinquefield. *Stocks, Bonds, Bills and Inflation 2002 Yearbook*. Chicago: Ibbotson Associates, 2003. When Roger Ibbotson first published this book it was revolutionary in that he painstakingly gathered data on investment performance that had not been readily available previously. While the data is no longer as unique as it once was, this is still a great source of historical performance information by asset class, published annually. See also, the "knowledge center," at www.ibbotson.com for a very wide array of scholarly articles on asset allocation and related topics.

Kurtz, Daniel L. *Managing Conflicts of Interest: Practical Guidelines for Nonprofit Boards*. Washington, DC: BoardSource, 2001. Attorney Daniel Kurtz helps board members understand exactly what constitutes a conflict of interest. He explains the legal context of the conflict, offers examples, and suggests guidelines on how to manage them. The book includes a diskette that contains sample conflict-of-interest policies and statements.

Lang, Andrew S. *Financial Responsibilities of Nonprofit Boards*. Washington, DC: BoardSource, 2003. Provide your board members with an understanding of their financial responsibilities, including an overview of financial oversight and ways to ensure against risk. Written in nontechnical language, this book will help your board understand financial planning, the IRS Form 990, and the audit process. Also included are financial board and staff job descriptions and charts on all the financial documents and reports, including due dates and filing procedures.

Malkiel, Burton. *A Random Walk Down Wall Street (8th Edition)*. New York: W.W. Norton and Company, 2003. Using the dot-com crash as an object lesson in how not to manage your portfolio, this book offers a gimmick-free and vastly informative guide to navigating the turbulence of the market and managing investments with confidence. With its life-cycle guide to investing, it matches the needs of investors at any age bracket, presenting a fair overview of traditional approaches to investing that are a proven success.

McLaughlin, Thomas A. *Financial Committees*. Washington, DC: BoardSource, 2004. Accountability is increasingly important to nonprofits, and every board must be engaged in understanding its fiduciary duties. Learn about the core responsibilities finance, audit, and investment committees can hold. Discover how these committees can address challenges in helping the rest of the board understand complicated fiscal issues. This book will also help finance committees to stress the importance of board member independence in oversight and audit functions, and prepare the board to address potential new legal regulations.

McLaughlin, Thomas A. *Presenting: Nonprofit Financials*. Washington, DC: BoardSource, 2001. *Presenting: Nonprofit Financials* is a ready-made on-screen presentation that can be used as a traditional graphics presentation, as overhead transparency slides, or printed out for handouts. Each slide is accompanied by a set of presentation notes and talking points to guide the discussion. Also included is a 12-page user's guide with suggestions for training board members on their financial responsibilities, instructions for using the presentation, and tips for providing proper fiduciary oversight.

Restatement of the Law Third, Trusts: Prudent Investor Rule. St. Paul, MN: American Law Institute Publishers, 1992. This is a useful publication for lawyers. The notes in this discussion of the trust law of investing are the best discussion of the legal history of the Prudent Investor Act to date.

Scott, David L. *Wall Street Words (3rd Edition).* Boston: Houghton Mifflin, 2003. *Wall Street Words* is an essential guide that is easy to use and especially useful for the non-professional. This updated edition has 4,500 entries — more than 700 of them newly added to reflect key developments in national and world markets — and covers everything from investment fundamentals to the sophisticated terminology of contemporary finance. Look for more than 100 case studies illustrating real-world investment examples and 50 insightful tips from industry professionals.

Trone, Donald B., William R. Albright, and Philip R. Taylor. *The Management of Investment Decisions.* McGraw-Hill: New York, 1996. This book provides the technical background to the Foundation for Fiduciary Studies' *Prudent Investment Practices,* discussed on page 84 of this book.

Unlocking Profit Potential: Your Organization's Guide to Social Entrepreneurship. Washington, DC: BoardSource and Community Wealth Ventures, 2002. Discover how to take a proactive approach to generating revenue through social entrepreneurship, conducting profitable enterprises to support the organization's ability to fulfill its mission. This resource discusses concepts of social entrepreneurship, available options, key issues, the role of board members, and guidelines for determining the best business venture for the organization.

About the Author

Robert P. Fry, Jr. is a financial advisor who works primarily with charitable organizations and the investors who support them. He is also an investment consultant to Merrill Lynch Trust Company and a member of the Trust Company's board of directors. He joined Merrill Lynch in 1997 as a Senior Philanthropic Consultant. In that capacity, he helped design and implement charitable giving strategies for high net worth individuals. Most recently, he was Director of Investments for Merrill Lynch Trust Company and the chairman of the investment committee on which he still serves.

Prior to Merrill Lynch, Mr. Fry was the Director of Charitable Services for Van Deventer & Hoch, Investment Counsel. While there, he assisted charitable organizations as a portfolio manager and consultant on the investment aspects of planned giving. He also spent more than 10 years in private practice as a business and securities law attorney.

Mr. Fry earned a Bachelor of Arts degree from the University of Southern California and a Juris Doctor degree from the University of California at Los Angeles. A participant in a number of community organizations, Bob most recently served for six years on the board of directors of the Christian Management Association. He is currently an active board member of Pura Vida Partners, a social enterprise coffee company.

Mr. Fry is a frequent seminar speaker at national events, including the AICPA Not for Profit Conference and the Investment Management Consultants Association (IMCA). He lives in Irvine, California, with his wife, son, and two daughters.

Bob Fry can be contacted by e-mail at rfryjr@aol.com.